Unit 1 Lifestyle

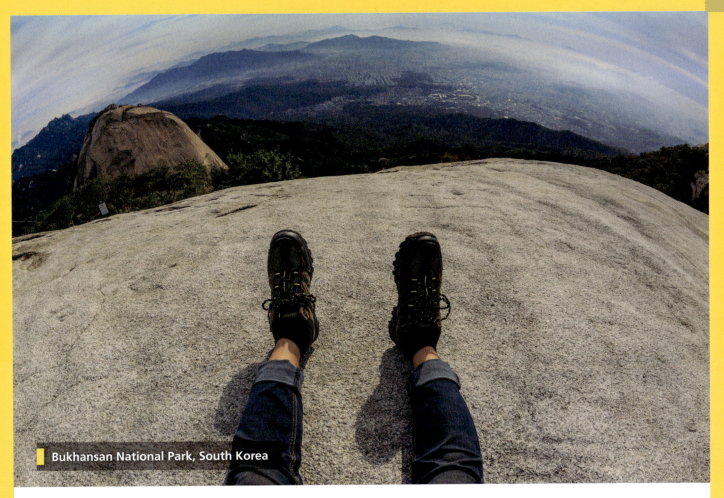

Bukhansan National Park, South Korea

FEATURES

10 How well do you sleep?

Complete a questionnaire about sleep

12 The secrets of a long life

How can you live to be one hundred?

14 Nature is good for you

Nature and health

18 Laughter yoga

A video about why laughing is good for you

1 Work in pairs. Describe the place in the photo. How do you think the person feels?

2 ▶1 Work in pairs. Listen to a description of the place in the photo. Answer the questions.

1 Where is Bukhansan National Park?
2 How many people visit it every year?
3 Why do they go there?

3 Look at the activities in the box. Which activities do you often do? When do you do them? Tell your partner.

take a bike ride	cook a meal
chat on social media	play sports and exercise
go for long walks	go fishing
play video games	play a musical instrument
read books	watch movies

I often go for long walks in the evening.

9

1a How well do you sleep?

Vocabulary everyday routines

1 Work in pairs. Match the two parts of the expressions for everyday routines. Then describe your typical day using some of the expressions.

1 get — ○ ○ asleep
2 fall ○ — ○ home late
3 take a ○ ○ TV
4 watch ○ ○ break

5 work long ○ ○ until midnight
6 wake up ○ ○ eight
7 get up about ○ ○ early
8 stay up ○ ○ hours

I often get home late from work …

Reading

2 Answer the questionnaire below. Then work in pairs and compare your answers.

3 Turn to page 153 and find out what your answers say about your lifestyle.

Grammar simple present and adverbs of frequency

4 Match the sentences (1–2) with their uses (a–b).

1 I work long hours and get home late.
2 The average human needs around eight hours of sleep per night.

a to talk about things that are always true ____
b to talk about habits and routines ____

> **SIMPLE PRESENT**

I/you/we/they **sleep.**	*He/she/it* **sleeps.**
I/you/we/they **don't sleep.**	*He/she/it* **doesn't sleep.**
Do *I/you/we/they* **sleep?**	**Does** *he/she/it* **sleep?**

For more information and practice, see page 156.

How well do you sleep?

1 **Do you often feel tired?**
A No, I never feel tired during the day.
B I sometimes feel tired after a long day at work.
C All the time! I'm always ready for bed.

2 **How many hours do you usually sleep at night?**
A Between seven and eight hours.
B More than nine. I rarely stay up late.
C Fewer than six.

3 **What do you usually do before you go to bed?**
A I watch TV or read a book.
B I exercise.
C I do some work.

4 **How long do you usually sleep on the weekends?**
A I usually sleep the same amount as any other day.
B I sometimes sleep for an extra hour or two.
C I always sleep until noon! I never get up early.

5 **How often do you wake up in the middle of the night?**
A I never wake up before morning.
B I rarely wake up more than once.
C Two or three times a night.

3A

**COMBO
SPLIT**

SECOND EDITION

LEARNING

JOHN HUGHES

HELEN STEPHENSON

PAUL DUMMETT

Australia · Brazil · Mexico · Singapore · United Kingdom · United States

Contents

Unit	Grammar	Vocabulary	Real life (functions)	Pronunciation
1 Lifestyle pages 9–20	simple present adverbs and expressions of frequency simple present and present continuous	everyday routines wordbuilding: collocations with *do*, *play*, and *go* word focus: *feel* medical problems	talking about illness	/s/, /z/, or /ɪz/ one or two syllables?
VIDEO: Laughter yoga **page 18** ▶ REVIEW **page 20**				
2 Competitions pages 21–32	modal verbs for rules *-ing* form	sports wordbuilding: suffixes word focus: *like*	talking about interests	/ŋ/ silent letters
VIDEO: Mongolian horse racing **page 30** ▶ REVIEW **page 32**				
3 Transportation pages 33–44	comparatives and superlatives *as … as* comparative modifiers	ways of traveling transportation nouns wordbuilding: compound nouns transportation adjectives transportation verbs taking transportation	going on a trip	*than* sentence stress intonation
VIDEO: Indian Railways **page 42** ▶ REVIEW **page 44**				
4 Challenges pages 45–56	simple past past continuous and simple past	risks and challenges personal qualities wordbuilding: verbs and nouns	telling a story	/d/, /t/, or /ɪd/ *was* / *were* intonation for responding
VIDEO: A microadventure **page 54** ▶ REVIEW **page 56**				
5 The environment pages 57–68	quantifiers articles: *a* / *an*, *the*, or no article	materials recycling results and figures word focus: *take*	calling about an order	/ðə/ or /ðiː/ sounding friendly
VIDEO: Recycling Cairo **page 66** ▶ REVIEW **page 68**				
6 Stages of life pages 69–80	infinitive forms future forms: *going to*, *will*, and present continuous	life events describing age celebrations word focus: *get* wordbuilding: synonyms	inviting, accepting, and declining	/tə/ contractions emphasizing words
VIDEO: Steel drums **page 78** ▶ REVIEW **page 80**				

COMMUNICATION ACTIVITIES **page 153** ▶ GRAMMAR SUMMARY **page 156** ▶ AUDIOSCRIPT **page 181**

Listening	Reading	Critical thinking	Speaking	Writing
someone talking about a national park near a city a radio interview about long life	a quiz about how well you sleep an article about centenarians an article about how nature is good for you	giving examples	finding out about lifestyle your current life making a town healthier	text type: filling out a form writing skill: information on forms
someone describing an Ironman competition three people talking about competitive sports in schools	an article about crazy competitions an article about female wrestlers in Bolivia	reading between the lines	explaining the rules of a sport or competition talking about your sports preferences your opinions about Olympic sports	text type: an ad writing skill: checking your writing
someone describing a photo two people discussing the pros and cons of different types of transportation a documentary about animal transportation	an article about solutions to transportation problems an article about the fate of the rickshaw in Kolkata, India	opinions for and against	talking about and comparing commutes advice on transportation a presentation about a pedicab company	text type: notes and messages writing skill: writing in note form
a caver talking about his hobby a climber makes an impossible decision	an article about two adventurers an article about different types of challenges	looking for evidence	talking about your past events you remember giving tips or advice on the best ways to learn English	text type: a short story writing skill: structure your writing
an excerpt from a documentary about a house made from recycled materials a news report about environmental projects	an article about e-waste an article about a boat made of plastic bottles	reading closely (part 1)	talking about recycling a general knowledge quiz changing attitudes and behaviors	a quiz text type: emails writing skill: formal words
differences between the generations a news item about Mardi Gras	an article about how a couple changed their lives an article about how Mardi Gras is celebrated around the world an article about coming-of-age ceremonies	analyzing the writer's view	plan the trip of a lifetime planning a celebration describing annual events	text type: a description writing skill: descriptive adjectives

Life around the world—in 12 videos

Unit 10 Wind turbines

Learn about an innovative product and how it can change lives.

Unit 11 The Golden Record

Voyager 1 carries a message for other life forms in the universe.

UK

USA

Unit 1 Laughter yoga

Find out why laughing is good for you.

Unit 6 Steel drums

Steelband music, or pan, is an important part of the culture in these Caribbean islands.

Trinidad & Tobago

Unit 7 My working life

Some people talk about their working lives.

Unit 9 Living in Venice

Learn what it's like to live in Venice.

Unit 2 Mongolian horse racing

Horse racing at a Mongolian festival.

Unit 8 Ancient languages, modern technology

Find out how technology is being used to record and preserve disappearing languages.

Unit 4 A microadventure

Two friends spend 24 hours in Croatia on a microadventure.

India

Unit 5 Recycling Cairo

Find out how recycled objects are used in Cairo.

Cambodia

Unit 12 Cambodia animal rescue

Rescuing victims of illegal animal poaching in Cambodia.

Unit 3 Indian Railways

Learn more about the Indian railway system.

Australia

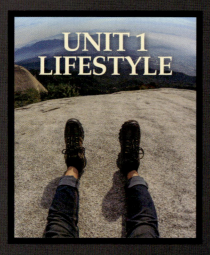

UNIT 1 LIFESTYLE

UNIT 2 COMPETITIONS

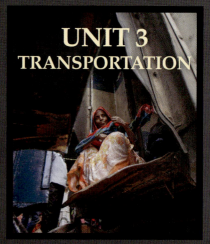

UNIT 3 TRANSPORTATION

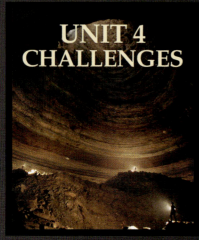

UNIT 4 CHALLENGES

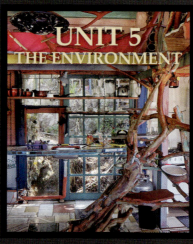

UNIT 5 THE ENVIRONMENT

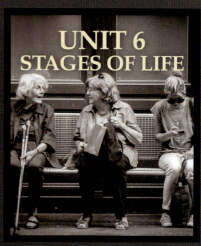

UNIT 6 STAGES OF LIFE

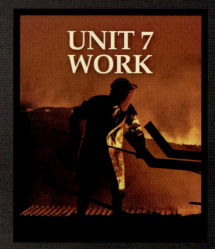

UNIT 7 WORK

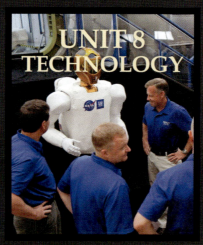

UNIT 8 TECHNOLOGY

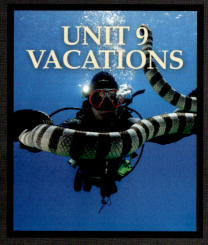

UNIT 9 VACATIONS

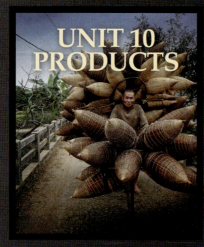

UNIT 10 PRODUCTS

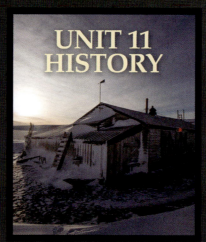

UNIT 11 HISTORY

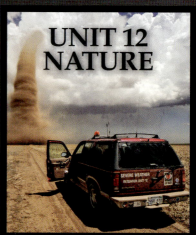

UNIT 12 NATURE

5 Look at the grammar box on page 10. Complete the article about sleep with the simple present form of the verbs in parentheses.

The secrets of sleep

Why ¹ _do we sleep_ (we / sleep)?
From birth, we ² _____ (spend) a third of our lives asleep, but scientists still ³ _____ (not / know) exactly why.
Why ⁴ _____ (we / have) problems sleeping?
In modern society, many adults ⁵ _____ (not / get) the seven or eight hours' sleep they need every night. We ⁶ _____ (work) long hours, and we rarely ⁷ _____ (go) to bed at sunset.
Why ⁸ _____ (we / sleep) differently?
It ⁹ _____ (depend) on the time of year and also our age. Teenagers usually ¹⁰ _____ (need) more sleep than adults. Lots of elderly people ¹¹ _____ (not / sleep) longer than four or five hours at night, but they often ¹² _____ (take) naps during the day.

6 Pronunciation /s/, /z/, or /ɪz/

▶ **3** Listen to the endings of these verbs. Is the sound /s/, /z/, or /ɪz/? Circle your answers. Then listen again and repeat.

1	feels	/s/ /z/ /ɪz/		5	goes	/s/ /z/ /ɪz/	
2	needs	/s/ /z/ /ɪz/		6	dances	/s/ /z/ /ɪz/	
3	watches	/s/ /z/ /ɪz/		7	does	/s/ /z/ /ɪz/	
4	sleeps	/s/ /z/ /ɪz/		8	works	/s/ /z/ /ɪz/	

7 Work in pairs. Discuss these questions.

1 What time do you and your friends usually get up? How late do you stay up?
2 Does anyone in your family ever take a nap in the afternoon?
3 Do people sleep longer in the summer or in the winter?

8 Look at the list below. Then underline the adverbs of frequency in the questionnaire on page 10 and write the missing adverbs in the list.

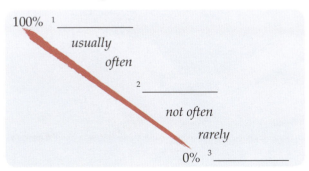

100% ¹ _____
    usually
      often
        ² _____
          not often
            rarely
0% ³ _____

▶ **ADVERBS and EXPRESSIONS OF FREQUENCY**

*She's **usually** late for work.*
*I **often** wake up at seven.*
*Do you **often** wake up in the middle of the night?*
*She wakes up **two or three times a night**.*
***Every month**, I visit my grandparents.*

For more information and practice, see page 156.

9 Look at the grammar box above. Circle the correct options to complete the rules (1–2).

1 An adverb of frequency usually goes *after / before* the main verb, but it goes *after / before* the verb *be*.
2 An expression of frequency (e.g., *twice a week*) usually goes *at the beginning / in the middle* or at the end of a sentence.

10 Show the correct place in the sentence for the adverb or expression in parentheses. Sometimes there is more than one correct answer.

1 My brother∕plays tennis on Saturday mornings. (always)
2 We eat at a restaurant. (about once a month)
3 I take a bus to school. (every day)
4 She is at home during the day. (rarely)
5 They go on vacation. (twice a year)
6 Are you late for work? (often)

Speaking **myLife**

11 Work in pairs. Find out about your partner's habits. Take turns asking questions with *How often …?* and the ideas in the box. Answer using an adverb or expression of frequency.

A: **How often do you eat** *out?*
B: About **once a month**.

go on vacation	be late for work/school
check your email	check your phone for messages
play board games	take public transportation
eat at a restaurant	feel stressed

12 Work in groups. Prepare a questionnaire about lifestyle for another group. Start each question with *How often …?, Are you often …?,* or *Do you often …?,* and offer three choices of answer (A, B, or C). Then ask your questions to the other group. Can you tell them what their answers say about their lifestyle?

1b The secrets of a long life

Reading

1 Work in pairs. Who is the oldest person you know? How old is he or she? How healthy is their lifestyle?

My grandfather is the oldest person I know. He's 83 and still plays golf.

2 Work in pairs. Read the article *The Secrets of a Long Life*. Answer the questions.

1. Why is Okinawa famous?
2. What kind of food do the people eat there?
3. Which of their activities do you do?
   I don't go fishing, but I do some gardening.

Wordbuilding collocations with *do, play,* and *go*

> ▶ **WORDBUILDING collocations with *do, play,* and *go***
>
> We use certain nouns with certain verbs. These are called collocations.
> *go fishing* NOT ~~*do fishing*~~ or ~~*play fishing*~~
>
> For more practice, see Workbook page 11.

3 Look at the wordbuilding box. Complete the chart below with activities from the article.

Do	Go	Play
	fishing	

4 Add these activities to the chart in Exercise 3. Use a dictionary if necessary.

cards	hiking	homework	nothing
running	shopping	tennis	the piano
yoga	soccer	karate	surfing

5 Work in pairs. Tell your partner about people you know using the collocations in the chart.

*My brother **does** karate. He's a black belt.*

▶ 4

The Secrets of a
Long Life

Okinawa in Japan has some of the oldest people in the world. It's famous for its high number of centenarians— men and women who live beyond one hundred years of age. Some of the reasons for their good health are that they:

- go fishing and eat what they catch.
- do a lot of gardening and grow their own fruit and vegetables.
- go cycling, and rarely drive when they can walk.
- often spend time with friends. They meet at people's houses and play games.
- exercise regularly, go swimming, and lead active lives.

An 89-year-old woman from Okinawa picks seaweed. It's part of her everyday food.

Listening

6 ▶ **5** Listen to a radio interview with photographer David McLain. Check (✓) the topics the speakers talk about.

☐ the age of men and women
☐ family life
☐ sleep
☐ food
☐ exercise

7 ▶ **5** Listen again. Are the sentences true (T) or false (F)?

1	David McLain is traveling to different countries.	T	F
2	He's talking to the radio announcer in the studio.	T	F
3	In Sardinia, men live to the same age as women.	T	F
4	Sardinian families rarely eat together.	T	F
5	Younger people are eating more unhealthy food, and they aren't exercising enough.	T	F

8 Work in pairs. Think about the lifestyle of people in your country. Is it similar to the lifestyle in Sardinia? How traditional is your country?

Grammar simple present and present continuous

9 Look at the grammar box and the sentences below from the interview. Which sentences use the simple present (S)? Which use the present continuous (C)?

1	Well, one man is trying to answer these questions— photographer David McLain.	S	C
2	He's speaking to us right now on the phone.	S	C
3	Men live to the same age as women.	S	C
4	Every Sunday, the whole family eats a big meal together.	S	C
5	Also, young people are moving to the city, so they are exercising less because of their lifestyle.	S	C

10 We use the present continuous to talk about something happening now or around now. Match the three present continuous sentences in Exercise 9 with the uses (a–c).

a to talk about a changing situation ____
b to talk about something happening around now, but not necessarily at this exact moment ____
c to talk about something actually in progress now ____

> ▶ **PRESENT CONTINUOUS**

I'm speak**ing**.
You/we/they're speak**ing**.
He/she/it's speak**ing**.

I'm not travel**ing**.
You/we/they **aren't** travel**ing**.
He/she/it **isn't** travel**ing**.

***Am** I* work**ing**?
***Are** you/we/they* work**ing**?
***Is** he/she/it* work**ing**?

For more information and practice, see page 156.

11 Complete the sentences with the simple present or present continuous form of these verbs.

reply	go	~~learn~~
read	spend	

1 We *'re learning* _____ a new language at the moment.
2 My friends and I often _____ time at each other's houses.
3 Can you wait a minute? I _____ to an email.
4 How often _____ you _____ to the gym?
5 I _____ a really interesting book at the moment.

Speaking *my* **Life**

12 Write pairs of questions. Use the simple present in one question and the present continuous in the other. Then work in pairs. Take turns asking and answering the questions.

1 a How / usually spend your free time?
How do you usually spend your free time?
  b / you / play / many sports these days?
Are you playing many sports these days?

2 a / often / read novels?
  _____
  b / read / any good books at the moment?
  _____

3 a Where / usually go on vacation?
  _____
  b Where / plan to go this year?
  _____

4 a / speak / any other languages?
  _____
  b / learn / any new languages?
  _____

1c Nature is good for you

Reading

1 Work in pairs. Look at the photo. Where do you think this woman is?

2 Read the article. Match the topics (a–c) with the paragraphs in the article (1–3).

    a how much time we spend outdoors ____
    b making nature part of city life   ____
    c studies by doctors   ____

3 Work in pairs. Read the article again. Answer the questions.

    1 What is the main change in how people spend their time?
    2 What is happening at national parks in Canada?
    3 After the math test, where did some people look at pictures of nature?
    4 What are they going to build in Dubai?
    5 In South Korea, how many people visit the new forests every year?

Word focus *feel*

4 Work in pairs. Underline four phrases with *feel* in the first paragraph of the article. Match the phrases to the uses (1–3).

    1 to talk about your emotions or health
    2 to talk about wanting to do something
    3 to talk about an opinion

5 Complete the questions with the words in the box.

about	better	like	that

    1 What do you usually feel _____ doing after a long day at work?
    2 Do you feel _____ nature is good for us? Why or why not?
    3 After a difficult day, what makes you feel _____ in the evening?
    4 How do you feel _____ nature?

6 Work in pairs. Take turns asking and answering the questions from Exercise 5.

A: What do you usually feel like doing after a long day at work?
B: Going for a run in my local park and then eating dinner. Sometimes I go out and meet friends.

Critical thinking giving examples

7 When writers give an opinion, they often support the idea with examples. Look at these sentences. Which sentence has the main idea (M)? Which sentences give examples (E)?

    a For example, the number of visitors to Canada's national parks is going down every year. M E
    b Humans are spending more time inside and less time outside. M E
    c And in countries such as the USA, only 10% of teenagers spend time outside every day. M E

8 Work in pairs. Read paragraphs 2 and 3 of the article. Find the sentence with the main idea and sentences with examples. Underline the phrases for giving examples.

For example, the number of visitors to Canada's national parks is going down every year.

9 Complete these sentences in your own words. Use examples from your own life. Then share your sentences with a partner.

    1 I relax in my free time in different ways. For example, …
    2 My hometown has some places with trees and nature, such as …
    3 There are some beautiful national parks in my country. A good example is …

Speaking my**Life**

10 Work in groups of four. Imagine your town has some money to make people's lives healthier. Look at the ideas below and think of one more.

- plant one hundred new trees in the town
- build a new park with a children's play area
- increase the number of bike paths across the town

11 Discuss the ideas in your group and choose the best one. Give reasons and examples.

I think increasing the number of bike paths is a good idea because cycling is good for your health and good for the environment.

NATURE
is good for you

1 How do you feel about nature? After spending hours indoors, do you often feel like going outside for a walk? Or if you work for hours at your desk, do you feel better when you take a break and visit your local
5 park? Most people think that nature is good for us; it's good for our bodies and good for our brains. However, humans are spending more time inside and less time outside. For example, the number of visitors to Canada's national parks is going down every
10 year. And in countries such as the USA, only 10% of teenagers spend time outside every day. Many doctors feel that this is a problem in the twenty-first century, and that it is making our physical health worse.

2 As a result, some doctors are studying the connection
15 between nature and health; one example of this is the work of Dr. Matilda van den Bosch in Sweden. The doctor gave two groups of people a math test. During the test, the heart rate[1] of people in both groups increased. After the test, one group of people sat in
20 a 3D-virtual-reality room with pictures and sounds of nature for fifteen minutes. Later, their heart rates were slower than the heart rates of people in the other group.

The virtual contact with nature helped these people feel more relaxed. Another good example of how nature
25 is good for health comes from Canada. In Toronto, researchers studied 31,000 people living in cities. Overall, they found that people who lived near parks were healthier.

3 Because of studies like these, some countries and cities
30 want nature to be part of people's everyday life. In Dubai, for example, there are plans for a new shopping mall with a large garden, so shoppers can relax outside with trees, plants, and water. In some countries— such as Switzerland—"forest schools" are popular;
35 schoolchildren study their subjects in the forest and do lots of exercise outside. And South Korea is another good example: It has new forests near its cities, and around 13 million people visit these forests every year. So after building cities for so long, perhaps it's now time
40 to start rebuilding nature.

[1] **heart rate** (n) /hɑrt reɪt/ the speed at which the heart beats (number of heartbeats per minute)

1d At the doctor's

Vocabulary medical problems

1 Look at the pictures. Match the people (1–8) with the medical problems (a–h).

a I have a headache.
b I have a backache.
c I have a runny nose.
d I have an earache.

e I have a stomachache.
f I have a temperature.
g I have a sore throat.
h I have a bad cough.

2 What do you do when you have the problems in Exercise 1? Discuss with a partner. Choose the best option (1–3) for each problem.

1 I go to bed.
2 I take medicine.
3 I go to the pharmacy or see my doctor.

3 Pronunciation one or two syllables?

▶ 7 Listen to these words. Which words have one syllable? Which words have two? Underline the stressed syllable in the two-syllable words. Then listen again and repeat.

ache	headache	ear	earache
stomach	throat	cough	backache

Real life talking about illness

4 ▶ 8 Work in pairs. Listen to two conversations, one at a pharmacy and one at a doctor's office. What medical problems does each person have?

5 ▶ 8 Listen again and write the number of the conversation (1 or 2) next to each piece of medical advice (a–e).

a Take this medicine three times a day. _1_

b Get some rest. ____

c Drink hot water with honey and lemon. ____

d Take one tablet twice a day. ____

e Buy cough drops. ____

6 Match the beginnings of the sentences (1–6) with their endings. Use the expressions for talking about illness to help you.

1	Do you have	○	○	this medicine.
2	You should take	○	○	see a doctor?
3	It's good for	○	○	a sore throat.
4	Why don't you	○	○	a headache?
5	I don't feel	○	○	well.
6	You need to	○	○	take these tablets.

> ▶ **TALKING ABOUT ILLNESS**
>
> **Asking and talking about illness**
> I don't feel very well.
> I feel sick/ill.
> Do you feel sick/ill?
> Do you have a temperature?
> How do you feel?
>
> **Giving advice**
> You need to / You should take this medicine.
> Why don't you buy some cough drops?
> It's good for a stomachache.
> Try drinking hot tea.
> If you still feel sick, then come back and see me again.

7 Work in pairs.

Student A: You have a medical problem. Choose one of the problems from Exercise 1 and tell Student B what your problem is.

Student B: You are a pharmacist. Ask how Student A feels and give advice.

Then change roles and have a new conversation.

1e Personal information

Writing filling out a form

1 Work in pairs. Discuss these questions.

- What kinds of forms do you sometimes fill out?
- Think of a form you filled out recently. What information did you write?

2 Work in pairs. Look at these forms. What is each form for?

A

Title	
First name	
Middle initial	
Last name	
Address	
Zip code	
Gender	
DOB	
No. of dependents	
Country of origin	
First language	

| Current occupation |
| |

| Do you smoke? |
| Yes ☐ No ☐ |
| Current medications |

| Details of past surgery or operations |
| |

B

PLEASE USE CAPITAL LETTERS

PASSPORT NO.   PLACE OF BIRTH

NATIONALITY   MARITAL STATUS

EDUCATION (DEGREE, ETC.)

Have you visited this country before? (If yes, give details)

Contact details of person in case of emergency (e.g., spouse, next of kin)

3 Writing skill information on forms

a Work in pairs. Match the questions (1–6) with the headings on the forms in Exercise 2 where you write the information.

1. Are you married, single, or divorced? *marital status*
2. Do you take any medicine?
3. How many children do you have?
4. What country were you born in?
5. Who can we call in your family if you need help?
6. What is the first letter of your middle name?

b Look at the forms again. Discuss these questions with your partner. Then check your answers on page 155.

1. How many abbreviations can you find in the forms? What do they mean?
   DOB = Date of birth
2. Under the heading *Title* on forms, we use the abbreviations *Mr.*, *Mrs.*, *Ms.*, and *Dr.* What do they mean?
3. Which form doesn't want you to write in lowercase letters?

4 Work in pairs. Design a form for new students at a language school.

- List all the information you need about the students.
- Then prepare the form.

5 Exchange your form with another pair. Use these questions to check their form.

- Is their form easy to fill out?
- Do you know what to write in each part?
- Would you change anything on the form?

1f Laughter yoga

Members of a laughter club meet by the seaside in Laguna Beach, California.

Before you watch

1 Work in pairs and answer these questions.

1 Think of someone you know who laughs a lot. Describe that person.
2 Do you laugh often? What makes you laugh?
3 Look at the photo and the caption. Why do you think people join this laughter club?

2 Key vocabulary

Read the sentences (1–6). The words and phrases in **bold** are used in the video. Write these words and phrases next to their definitions (a–f).

1 I heard a funny **joke** yesterday.
2 Exercise is a good **way** to relieve stress.
3 The doctors performed an operation to clear a blockage in the **blood vessels** that supply his heart.
4 One of the **benefits** of yoga is increased muscle strength and tone.
5 There are about 50 **calories** in an apple.
6 If you take in 2,500 calories a day, and **burn** 2,500 calories a day, you'll stay at about the same weight.

a good or helpful results or effects
  _____
b a method, style, or manner of doing something _____
c units used to measure the amount of energy that food provides
  _____
d the narrow tubes through which your blood flows _____
e use up _____
f something said to cause laughter
  _____

3 You are going to watch members of a laughter club doing laughter yoga. What do you think the members do during their laughter yoga session? Check (✓) the items you think are true.

☐ They walk around and greet one another.
☐ They watch a funny movie.
☐ They make eye contact with other members.
☐ They chant and clap their hands.
☐ They take funny photos on their cell phones.
☐ They all do the same body movements while laughing.

While you watch

4 ▶ **1.1** Watch the video. Were your predictions in Exercise 3 correct?

5 ▶ **1.1** Watch the video again. Are these sentences true (T) or false (F)?

1	The people in the video are laughing because someone told a joke.	T	F
2	Laughter yoga helps people feel happier through laughing.	T	F
3	When you laugh, changes happen in your body.	T	F
4	Laughing can help you lose weight.	T	F

6 ▶ **1.1** Watch the video again. Choose the correct option (a or b) to complete each sentence.

1 Laughing can make your blood vessels _____ .
  a cleaner   b wider
2 Laughing can reduce the risk of _____ .
  a heart disease   b certain cancers
3 You can burn _____ calories when you laugh for five to ten minutes.
  a 40   b 400
4 We start laughing when we are around _____ .
  a one month old   b three months old

After you watch

7 Vocabulary in context

▶ **1.2** Watch the clips from the video. Choose the correct meaning of the words and phrases.

8 Work in pairs and answer these questions.

1 Would you join a laughter club? Why or why not?
2 Do you think laughter is better than other forms of exercise? Give examples to support your answer.

Grammar

1 Circle the correct options to complete the text about a man named Nazroo.

Every day, Nazroo ¹ *works / is working* with elephants. In this photo, ² *he takes / he's taking* his favorite elephant, Rajan, for a swim. ³ *They swim / They're swimming* in the ocean around the Andaman Islands. Sometimes they ⁴ *like / are liking* to relax this way after a hard day. Rajan ⁵ *doesn't seem / isn't seeming* worried about being underwater. I suppose ⁶ *it feels / it is feeling* good after a long, hot day at work.

2 Show the correct place in the sentence for the expression in parentheses. In three sentences, there is more than one correct answer.

1 I play video games. (rarely)
2 We're studying Spanish. (at the moment)
3 My family plays sports. (every weekend)
4 All my friends are working. (these days)

3 **>> MB** Rewrite the sentences in Exercise 2 so they are true for you.

I CAN	
talk about everyday routines	☐
use adverbs and expressions of frequency	☐

Vocabulary

4 Match the verbs in A with the words in B. Then complete the sentences with the expressions.

A	fall	take	work
B	long hours	asleep	a break

1 I can't _____ _____ because of all the noise outside my bedroom.
2 At work, we always _____ _____ at 11 and have coffee.
3 We all _____ _____ these days because there is a lot to do.

5 Which words can follow the verb in **bold**? Cross out the incorrect word.

1 **do** homework, housework, ~~relaxing~~, yoga
2 **go** asleep, surfing, jogging, home
3 **play** golf, swimming, games, tennis
4 **feel** tired, happy, ache, sick

6 **>> MB** Work in pairs. Write four sentences using verbs from Exercises 4 and 5, but leave out the verb.

We often _____ yoga when we wake up.

Then work with another pair. Take turns reading your sentences and guessing the missing word.

I CAN	
describe daily routines	☐
talk about free-time activities	☐

Real life

7 Circle the correct options to complete the conversation between two friends.

A: ¹ *How do / Do* you feel?
B: Not very ² *well / ill*. I have a ³ *pain / sore* throat.
A: ⁴ *Do you feel / Do you have* a temperature?
B: I don't know. I feel a little hot.
A: ⁵ *Try / You need* drinking some honey and lemon in hot water.
B: Good idea.
A: But you ⁶ *should / it's a good idea* also see your doctor.

8 **>> MB** Work in pairs. Look at the pictures and answer the questions.

1 What medical problems do these people have?
2 What advice can you give them?
You should go to bed.

I CAN	
talk about medical problems and illness	☐
give advice	☐

Unit 2 Competitions

Athletes in Cozumel, Mexico, compete for a place in the Ironman championship.

FEATURES

22 Crazy competitions!

Making rules for new competitions

24 Winning and losing

Is competition important in sports?

26 Bolivian wrestlers

Women competing in a national sport

30 Mongolian horse racing

A video about horse racing at a Mongolian festival

1 Work in pairs. Look at the photo and the caption. What do you know about this kind of competition?

2 ▶9 Listen to someone talking about the Ironman competition. Work in pairs. Answer the questions.

   1 How many races are there in the Ironman competition?
   2 How many kilometers do the competitors swim and cycle?
   3 How many people compete in Hawaii every year?

3 The words in the box are from the same family. Which word is:

   1 a verb?   3 a noun (thing)?
   2 an adjective?   4 a noun (person)?

   | competitor | competitive | competition | compete |

4 Complete the questions with the words from the box above. Then ask and answer the questions with a partner.

   1 In sports, are you normally a _____ or a spectator?
   2 Do you ever _____ in sports?
   3 What types of _____ do you like?
   4 Are you a _____ person? Why or why not?

2a Crazy competitions!

Reading

1 Work in pairs. Look at the title of the article and the two photos. Why do you think these competitions are "crazy"?

2 Read the article and match the sentences (1–6) with the competitions (A or B). Two sentences are true for both competitions.

1 Competitors start and end at the same place. _A_
2 The rules are similar to those of another real sport. ____
3 The competition is held once a year. ____
4 It involves a type of transportation. ____
5 It's for teams. ____
6 There is a time limit. ____

3 Which of the two competitions would you like to watch or take part in? Do you have any crazy competitions in your country? Discuss with a partner.

Vocabulary sports

4 Look at the highlighted words in the article. Use these words to complete the sentences below.

1 Runners at the Olympic Games get a gold medal when they win a _____ .
2 In soccer, there are eleven _____ on each side.
3 A baseball _____ is played between two _____ .
4 How many _____ did you score?
5 After two hours of running, the _____ was finally in sight.
6 The _____ received a gold medal.

5 Work in pairs. Answer these questions.

1 How many different kinds of races can you think of?
2 What is your favorite team sport? How many players are there in a team?
3 What are the names of the sports teams in your town or city?
4 In what games do you score goals and in what games do you score points?

▶ 10

CRAZY COMPETITIONS!

There are lots of competitions in the USA, and some of them are a bit crazy!

A The Idiotarod

The Idiotarod is an annual race in twenty different US cities. Each team must have five people and a shopping cart. One person usually rides in the cart, and four people pull it. Teams can decorate the shopping cart, but they can't change the wheels. All the teams have to start and finish at the same place, but they don't have to run on the same roads. The members of each team must cross the finish line together, and they can't finish without the cart!

B The Mud Bowl Championship

Mud Bowl football—played every September in North Conway, New Hampshire, USA—is similar to regular American football, in that players can pick up the ball and run with it. There are also two teams, but the game is shorter. The winner is the team with the most points at the end of sixty minutes. The really big difference is that the players have to play in a field with half a meter of mud!

Grammar modal verbs for rules

6 Look at the sentences in the grammar box. Complete the explanations (a–d) with the modal verbs in **bold** in the grammar box.

a We use _____ or _____ when the rules say it's necessary.

b We use _____ when it's allowed by the rules.

c We use _____ when something isn't necessary but is allowed by the rules.

d We use _____ when it isn't allowed by the rules.

7 Circle the correct options to complete the sentences about different sports.

1 Do you *have to / must* wear a helmet when you play ice hockey?

2 In tennis, players *don't have to / can* use video replay technology if they want to see where the ball landed. This technology has transformed the game of tennis.

3 In bowling, you can bring your own ball, but you *have to / don't have to* if you don't want to.

4 Soccer players *must / don't have to* follow the rules, or the referee will send them off the field. They *have to / can't* argue with the referee.

8 Complete the description of another competition with these modal verbs. Use each modal verb only once.

~~must~~	have to	don't have to	can't	can

Every two years, people from all over the globe enter the World Beard and Moustache Championships. The rules are simple. You ¹___*must*___ be over eighteen years old, and you ²_____ have a moustache or a beard, or both. Also, you ³_____ put on false hair! In total, there are eighteen different categories, but competitors ⁴_____ only enter one category. There are categories for short beards and different moustaches, so you ⁵_____ have the longest moustache or the biggest beard to win a prize.

Speaking my Life

9 Work in pairs. You are going to explain the rules of a sport or competition. Choose one of the following. Make a list of six to seven rules. Then explain your rules to another pair.

- a popular sport in your country
- a popular TV quiz show or TV competition
- an annual national or international competition

*Baseball is a popular sport in my country. You **have to** play with two teams, a ball, and a bat.*

2b Winning and losing

Wordbuilding suffixes

1 Are any of the athletes in the photos famous in your country? Match the people (A–C) with these words.

> tennis player _____   runner _____
> soccer player _____

> ▶ **WORDBUILDING suffixes**
>
> You can add *-er* to some sports to describe the person who plays the sport:
> ski → skier, golf → golfer
> You can add *player* to some sports:
> tennis → tennis player, baseball → baseball player
> Some sports don't use the suffix *-er* or *player*:
> athletics → athlete, cycle → cyclist
>
> For more practice, see Workbook page 19.

2 Work in pairs. Look at the wordbuilding box. What is the word for a person who:

1 boxes? *boxer*   5 plays chess?
2 motorcycles?   6 drives a racing car?
3 plays basketball?   7 does gymnastics?
4 swims?   8 goes surfing?

3 Work in pairs. Who are the most famous athletes in your country? What type of athlete are they? (e.g., *a swimmer, a golfer, a skateboarder*)

Lionel Messi is very famous in my country. He's a soccer player.

Listening

4 Read the quotes with the photos. Do you think winning is always important in sports? Why or why not? Discuss with a partner.

5 ▶ 11 Listen to three people talking about competitive sports in schools. Match the speakers (1–3) with their opinions (a–c).

a Speaker _____ thinks non-competitive sports are a good idea.
b Speaker _____ thinks competitive sports are a good idea in schools.
c Speaker _____ thinks sports in schools are a good idea, but there can be problems.

A "I don't like losing." Usain Bolt

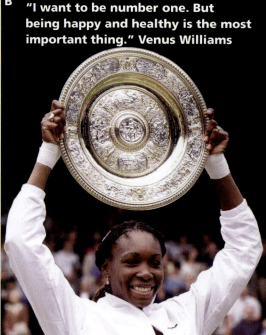

B "I want to be number one. But being happy and healthy is the most important thing." Venus Williams

C "You can't win all the time." Lionel Messi

6 Look at these opinions for and against competitive sports in schools. Which are the opinions for (F) and which are the opinions against (A)?

1 Winning and losing teaches students about life. Ⓕ A
2 A lot of successful schools don't have competitive sports. F A
3 Children get more exercise when they try to win. F A
4 Winning isn't important as long as you do your best. F A
5 Children learn to work well in teams when they play against other teams. F A
6 Students learn to work hard by doing competitive sports. F A
7 Some parents don't like losing and get angry with their children. F A
8 All children are different, and some aren't good at sports. F A
9 Competitive sports are fun. F A

7 ▶ 11 Which opinions (1–9) from Exercise 6 does each speaker give? Listen again and check.

Speaker 1 ___*1,*___
Speaker 2 _____
Speaker 3 _____

8 Work in groups. Discuss the opinions in Exercise 6. Answer these questions.

1 Which opinions do you agree with?
2 Which do you disagree with?
3 Are there any other reasons for or against competitive sports in schools?

Grammar *-ing* form

▶ **-ING FORM**

1 ***Learning*** to win and lose is important in a child's education.
2 Competitive sports in schools are good for ***teaching*** children the value of teamwork.
3 Some parents hate ***losing***.

For more information and practice, see page 158.

9 Look at the grammar box. The verbs in the *-ing* form are in **bold**. Match these verbs (1–3) with the uses of the *-ing* form (a–c).

a It is the subject of the sentence. ____
b It comes after a verb (e.g., *like*). ____
c It comes after a preposition (e.g., *of*).
____

10 Work in pairs. Put the words in the correct order to make quotes by famous athletes. Then match the *-ing* forms with the uses (a–c) in Exercise 9.

1 never / thought / losing / of / I
   (Muhammad Ali, boxer)
2 love / I just / winning
   (Ayrton Senna, race car driver)
3 a champion / afraid / losing / isn't / of
   (Billie Jean King, tennis player)
4 hate / I / losing
   (Sachin Tendulkar, cricket player)
5 I'm / more worried about / a good person / being / than being the best soccer player
   (Lionel Messi, soccer player)

11 ▶ 12 Circle the correct options to complete this conversation. Then listen and check.

A: What's on TV?
B: ¹*Cycle / Cycling*. It's the Tour de France. I love ²*watch / watching* it.
A: Oh, no! I ³*think / thinking* it's boring!
B: I disagree. I really enjoy ⁴*watch / watching* the cyclists ride through the mountains.
A: ⁵*Sit / Sitting* in front of the TV all day isn't exciting. I'm tired of ⁶*do / doing* nothing. Are you any good at tennis? We could ⁷*play / playing* this afternoon.
B: But I want to ⁸*watch / watching* this.
A: What's wrong? Are you afraid of ⁹*lose / losing*?

12 Pronunciation /ŋ/

a ▶ 13 Listen to six words. Circle the word you hear.

1	thin	think	thing
2	win	wink	wing
3	ban	bank	bang
4	sin	sink	sing
5	ran	rank	rang
6	pin	pink	ping

b ▶ 12 Listen again to the conversation from Exercise 11. Notice the pronunciation of the *-ing* forms. Then work in pairs and practice the conversation.

Speaking my Life

13 Work in pairs. Ask questions to find out what sports or activities your partner likes. Then complete the sentences.

A: *What sports do you **love watching**?*
B: *Tennis. What about you?*

1 I love watching _____ , but my partner doesn't.
2 I think _____ is boring, but my partner loves it!
3 We both enjoy _____ , but we hate _____ .
4 I'm good at _____ , but my partner isn't.

2c Bolivian wrestlers

Reading

1 Work in pairs. Discuss the questions.

1 Do many people watch boxing or wrestling in your country?
2 Why do some people dislike these types of sports?
3 What do you think about these sports?

2 Read the article about wrestling in Bolivia. Which paragraph (1–5) describes:

a the two wrestlers before the fight? __2__
b the popularity of male and female wrestling in Bolivia? ____
c Yolanda's family life? ____
d the reason why a fan watches it? ____
e the fight between the two wrestlers? ____

3 Find words in the article for these definitions.

1 something people watch for pleasure
  e_ntertainment_
2 a large group of people
  c_____
3 the person who describes the action in a sport
  c_____
4 get very excited, shout, and jump up and down
  g_____ c_____
5 people who like a famous athlete
  f_____
6 the money you earn for work done
  s_____

Critical thinking reading between the lines

4 An article doesn't always tell us about how people feel, but we can often guess. Match the people from the article (1–3) with the sentences (a–c).

1 Yolanda
2 Yolanda's daughter
3 Esperanza

a "I don't understand why wrestling is so popular." ____
b "I feel wonderful every time I step into the ring." ____
c "Life is very hard for people like me." ____

5 Work in pairs. Discuss these questions.

1 How do you feel about the women wrestlers?
2 Would you like to see this sport? Why or why not?

Word focus *like*

6 The word *like* has a number of meanings and uses. Match the sentences (1–4) with the uses (a–d).

a We use *like* + noun to talk about things we enjoy.
b We use *like* + -*ing* to talk about activities we enjoy doing.
c We use *be/look like* to talk about similarities between people/things/actions.
d We use *would like to* + base form of a verb to talk about future plans or ambitions.

1 Most people **like** soccer. ____
2 Yolanda and Claudina **are like** famous pop stars. ____
3 **Would** your daughters **like to** become wrestlers one day? ____
4 Esperanza **likes** watching wrestling. ____

7 Match the questions with *like* (1–5) with their answers (a–e).

1 What do you like doing on the weekend?
2 What kind of music do you like?
3 Are you like anyone in your family?
4 Where would you like to go on your next vacation?
5 What does your dad look like?

a Yeah, I'm really similar to my mom. ____
b Spain. Or Portugal, maybe. ____
c Anything. Rock, classical—I don't mind. ____
d Going to the movies. ____
e He's tall and has brown hair. ____

8 Work in pairs. Take turns asking the questions from Exercise 7 and giving your own answers.

Speaking myLife

9 Work in groups. Can you name ten sports in the Olympic Games?

10 These six sports are not in the Olympic Games. Discuss the questions in your group and give reasons for your answers.

| American football | bowling | cricket |
| mixed martial arts | darts | squash |

1 Which of the six sports do you think is the most popular?
2 Which three sports would your group like to have at the next Olympics?

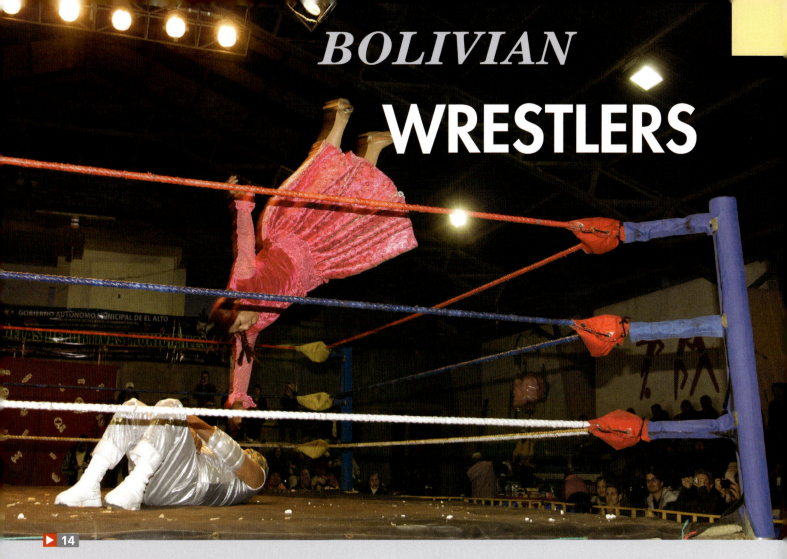

BOLIVIAN WRESTLERS

▶ 14

1 In Bolivia, soccer is the national sport, but the country is also famous for another sport—wrestling. Local people like watching wrestling, and it's popular with tourists, too. It's an exciting mixture of sport, drama, and entertainment. When modern wrestling started in Bolivia in the 1950s, the competitors were all men, but nowadays women are also competing in the ring.

2 The city of El Alto is a good place to watch wrestling. Hundreds of spectators go to the fights in the evening. This evening, the crowd is sitting around a huge wrestling ring and shouting, "Bring them on! Bring them on!" Suddenly, the commentator is speaking into a microphone, "Ladies and gentlemen. It's time for Yolanda and Claudina!" The crowd is screaming with excitement as two women in colorful clothes enter the ring.

3 Yolanda and Claudina are like famous pop stars. They smile and wave to their fans. The music stops, and the referee starts the fight. Claudina jumps on Yolanda.

Then Yolanda throws Claudina on the floor. As Claudina lies on the floor, Yolanda smiles and waves to the crowd. Then Claudina gets up and pushes Yolanda onto the ground. One minute, Yolanda is winning. The next minute, Claudina is winning. The spectators go crazy!

4 Away from the ring, many wrestlers are women with families. At home, Yolanda has a normal, quiet family life. She has two daughters, and she makes clothes for a living. Her father was also a wrestler, so it's a family tradition. In answer to the question "Would your daughters like to become wrestlers one day?", Yolanda says they wouldn't. She answers, "My daughters ask me why I do this. It's dangerous, and they complain that wrestling doesn't bring any money into the house." So why does she do it?

5 Yolanda loves wrestling because of her fans—and she has lots of them. One of her fans is named Esperanza Cancina. Esperanza pays $1.50 (a large part of her salary) to sit near the ring. She likes watching wrestling because, she says, "We laugh and we forget our problems for three or four hours."

2d Joining a group

Speaking

1 Work as a class or in groups. Interview different people. Find someone who:

1 is a member of a team or club.
2 has to go to regular meetings (e.g., every week).
3 competes with their team or club.

Real life talking about interests

2 Work in pairs. Look at the ads below. Would you like to join one of these clubs? Why or why not?

A | Would you like to **get fit** and **make new friends?** | Join our running groups for beginners and for more experienced runners. It's non-competitive and fun.

7 p.m. every Wednesday.

Call Mike for details at 415-555-2671.

B *Join us and* **WIN** *a new camera!*

The Barton Photography Club welcomes new members. We are a busy club with regular speakers. Join before March 1st and enter our summer photography competition. First prize is a new XP8ii camera! The entry fee is $15 (including membership).

Visit www.bartonphotoclub.com to join.

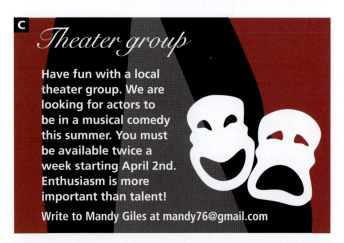

C *Theater group*

Have fun with a local theater group. We are looking for actors to be in a musical comedy this summer. You must be available twice a week starting April 2nd. Enthusiasm is more important than talent!

Write to Mandy Giles at mandy76@gmail.com

3 ▶ 15 Two people are looking at the ads (from Exercise 2) in their local newspaper. Listen to their conversation. Number the ads (A–C) in the order they are discussed (1–3).

A ____   B ____   C ____

4 ▶ 15 Listen again and complete these sentences with the words you hear.

1 You're really _____ taking photos.
2 Well, _____ joining something else?
3 Are you _____ acting?
4 I _____ standing up in front of people.
5 I'm _____ good at singing.
6 You should _____ . I think you'd enjoy it.
7 I think I'd _____ join this one on Wednesday evenings.
8 It _____ like fun. _____ you come, too?

5 Work in pairs. Match the sentences in Exercise 4 with the three categories in the box below.

6 Pronunciation silent letters

▶ 16 Some letters in English words are not pronounced. Listen to these words from the conversation and cross out the silent letters. Then listen again and repeat.

1 interested   4 could
2 should   5 what
3 friends   6 whole

7 Work in pairs. What other clubs would you like to join? Why would you like to join them?

2e Advertising for members

Writing an ad

1 Work in small groups. What makes a good ad and a bad ad? Think about ads you like and don't like in magazines, on TV, or online.

2 Read the advice about how to write effective ads. Then look at the ads on page 28. Discuss these questions as a group.

    1 Which ad follows most of the advice?
    2 How could you improve the ads?

> ### *How to* WRITE EFFECTIVE ADS
>
> - Start with a good headline. You could ask a question or solve a problem.
> - The ad should explain the reasons for buying something or joining a club.
> - If possible, offer something for free or a prize.
> - Include any other important information (dates, times, location, contact information, etc.).
> - Photos, pictures, or images always help.

3 Work in pairs. You are going to plan a new club. Discuss these questions.

    1 What type of club is it?
    2 Who is the club for?
    3 Are there any rules for members?
    4 Is there a membership fee? How much is it?
    5 Where and how often will it meet?

4 Plan and write an ad for your club.

5 Writing skill checking your writing

a It is important to check your writing for mistakes before people read it. Read these sentences (1–8) from ads and find one mistake in each sentence. Circle the mistake and write the correct symbol from the correction key. Each key is used once.

    1 Would you like to learn a musical instrument.? __P__
    2 Enter our exciteing competition! ____
    3 Are you good at play tennis? ____
    4 We meet at Tuesdays and Thursdays. ____
    5 It's fun way to get fit. ____
    6 Join this club new! ____
    7 Get healthy and play yoga. ____
    8 Call peter at 077 237 5980. ____

Writing correction key		
Sp	=	spelling mistake
MW	=	missing word
P	=	punctuation mistake
Prep	=	preposition mistake
Gr	=	grammar mistake
WO	=	word order mistake
C	=	capital letter mistake
WW	=	wrong word

b Read your ad from Exercise 4 again. Are there any mistakes?

6 Display your ads around the classroom. Walk around and read about each other's new clubs. Think about these questions.

- Which clubs would you like to join?
- Which ads are effective? Why?

2f Mongolian horse racing

Children compete in a horse race at the Naadam festival, Mongolia.

Before you watch

1 Work in pairs. Look at the photo of horse racing in Mongolia. Answer these questions.

1 Do you have horse racing in your country?
2 How popular is it as a sport?

2 Key vocabulary

Read the sentences (1–7). The words and phrases in **bold** are used in the video. Write these words and phrases next to their definitions (a–g).

1 In the Olympic Games, each winner receives a gold **medal**.
2 I got 100% on the exam, so I feel very **proud** of myself.
3 A religious man **blesses** people.
4 My horse can run **like the wind**.
5 At the festival, there were **displays** by actors and performers.
6 A typical **rodeo** includes events such as bull riding and catching cows with ropes.
7 In this competition, I have one main **rival** who always tries to beat me.

a asks a god (or gods) to protect something or someone _____
b pleased because you've done something well _____
c shows or presentations _____
d a metal disc given for an achievement _____
e very quickly _____
f a competition where cowboys show different skills _____
g a person who is as good or almost as good as you at doing something _____

While you watch

3 ▶ **2.1** Watch the video. Number these actions in the order you see them (1–6).

____ Mukhdalai's horse wins the race.
____ The riders leave the starting point.
_1_ A religious woman blesses the horses.
____ Mukhdalai receives first prize.
____ A horse rider picks up poles.
____ Two men wrestle.

4 ▶ **2.1** Watch the video again. Choose the correct option (a or b) to complete each sentence.

1 The Naadam is a Mongolian _____ festival.
 a spring
 b summer
2 Mukhdalai and Namjin are horse _____ who compete against each other.
 a riders
 b trainers
3 Mukhdalai and Namjin _____ each other.
 a like
 b don't like
4 There are about _____ horses competing in the race.
 a twenty
 b eighty
5 The starting point is at the _____ .
 a top of a hill
 b bottom of a valley
6 _____ is wearing green and white.
 a Mukhdalai's son
 b Namjin's son
7 Mukhdalai's horse is in first place for _____ race.
 a the whole
 b part of the
8 It is Namjin's horse's _____ race.
 a first
 b fifth

After you watch

5 Vocabulary in context

a ▶ **2.2** Watch the clips from the video. Choose the correct meaning of the words and phrases.

b Work in pairs. Ask and answer these questions.

1 What are some annual celebrations in your country?
2 Imagine you and your classmates are competing in a 100-meter race. Who do you think will take the lead and win? Do you think this person will finish a long way ahead of the rest?

6 Work in pairs. Write five questions about the Naadam festival in the video.

What is the Naadam festival famous for?

7 Work with a new partner. Take turns asking and answering your questions from Exercise 6 about the Naadam.

Grammar

1 Circle the correct options to complete the text about an unusual competition.

The first bed race was in Knaresborough, UK, in 1966. The rules are simple. Each team [1] *can / has to* race with one bed on wheels. There are six people to a team and one passenger. The team [2] *must / doesn't have to* have either six men or six women, or you [3] *can / can't* also race with a team of three men and three women. The passenger [4] *has to / doesn't have to* be an adult, but he or she [5] *doesn't have to / can't* be younger than twelve years old. The time limit for the race is thirty minutes, and you [6] *can't / have to* take longer.

2 **≫ MB** Work in pairs. What sports do these people play? Describe two rules for each sport.

Venus Williams	Lionel Messi	Usain Bolt

3 Complete the sentences with the *-ing* form of these verbs.

go	learn	lose	watch	win

1 _____ to speak another language is very useful.
2 Peter is very competitive—he hates _____ .
3 Trying is more important than _____ .
4 I think _____ to a basketball game is more fun than _____ it on TV.

4 **≫ MB** Complete the sentences in your own words using the *-ing* form. Then tell a partner.

1 _____ is very good for you.
2 I'm really interested in _____ .
3 I don't like _____ .

I CAN	
use modal verbs for rules	☐
use the *-ing* form	☐

Vocabulary

5 Write the missing vowels in these words related to sports. Race with a partner to see who can finish first.

1 r__c__
2 g__ __ls
3 cr__wd
4 g__me
5 f__n__sh l__n__
6 b__s__b__ll
7 w__nn__r
8 f__ns
9 t__ __m
10 b__x__r

6 Work in pairs. Answer these questions with four of the words from Exercise 5.

1 What do you have to cross in a race?
2 What is the opposite of *a loser*?
3 What type of competition is Formula One?
4 What do you call a group of people who like an athlete or a sports team?

7 **≫ MB** Work in pairs. Choose three more words from Exercise 5 and write three questions for them. Then work with another pair and take turns asking and answering your questions.

I CAN	
talk about sports and athletes	☐

Real life

8 Complete the conversation. Write one word in each blank.

A: Are you interested [1] _____ painting? There's a new evening class at my college.
B: But I'm not very good [2] _____ art.
A: I'm not either, but I'd like [3] _____ learn. Come on. You should do it [4] _____ me.
B: Sorry. What about doing something else?
A: [5] _____ you like taking photos? There's also a class for that.
B: Actually, that sounds interesting.

9 **≫ MB** Complete these sentences in your own words. Then share your sentences with a partner.

1 I'm good at …
2 I think I'd enjoy learning …
3 I'm also interested in …
4 I wouldn't like to …

I CAN	
talk about my interests	☐

Unit 3 Transportation

Taking the train in Dhaka, Bangladesh

FEATURES

34 Transportation solutions

Find out about some new transportation ideas

36 Transportation around the world

Comparing different types of transportation

38 The end of the road

How much longer can the rickshaw survive?

42 Indian Railways

A video about one of the world's largest transportation networks

1 Work in pairs. Look at the photo. Where is the woman? Why do you think she is traveling like this?

2 ▶ 17 Listen to someone talking about the photo. Why isn't the woman inside the train?

3 Work in pairs. Which ways of traveling would you prefer for the activities (1–7)? Give your reasons.

by bicycle	by bus	by truck	by plane
by train	in my car	in a taxi	on a ferry
on foot	on a motorcycle	on a ship	

1 visit relatives
   *I'd prefer to **visit** my **relatives by bicycle** or **on foot** because they only live five minutes from my house.*
2 move house and furniture
3 get to the airport
4 cross an ocean
5 go out in the evening to a party or restaurant
6 commute to school or work
7 go shopping

3a Transportation solutions

Reading

1 Read the article about three solutions to transportation problems. Match the paragraphs with the photos (1–3).

Paragraph A ____
Paragraph B ____
Paragraph C ____

2 Look at the photos and read the article again. Which types of transportation do the sentences (1–4) describe? Match the sentences to a–c below. Some sentences describe more than one type.

1 It moves over people's heads.
2 It's a faster way to commute.
3 It's environmentally friendly.
4 It's good for long distances.

a driverless cars _____
b monorail __*1,*____
c Hyperloop __*1,*____

Vocabulary transportation nouns

> **WORDBUILDING compound nouns**
>
> We can join two words to make a new noun: *bus + stop = bus stop*, *air + port = airport* , *down + town = downtown*
> A compound noun can be two words (*bus stop*) or one word (*airport*).
>
> For more practice, see Workbook page 27.

3 Find the compound nouns in **bold** in the article. Match them with their definitions (1–6).

1 the maximum speed you can legally drive ___*speed limit*___
2 a long line of vehicles moving slowly on the road _____
3 the time of day when lots of people travel to/from work _____
4 the money you spend on gas for transportation _____
5 the amount of CO_2 that a type of transportation produces _____
6 the main or central part of a city _____

4 Work in pairs. Discuss these questions.

1 Which of the three transportation solutions in the article do you think are a good idea?
2 Which traffic problems could they solve in your area?

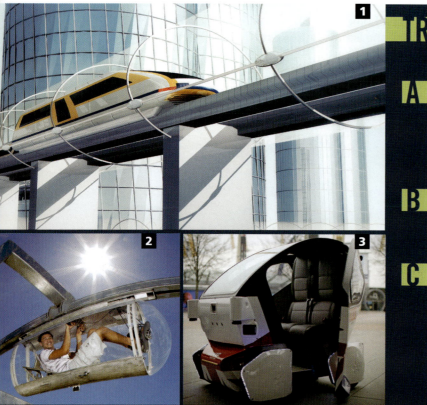

TRANSPORTATION SOLUTIONS

▶ 18

A BMW, Volvo, General Motors, and Google are all currently working on driverless cars. Some driverless cars use solar energy, which reduces **fuel costs** and lowers **carbon emissions**. They are also safer because the computer controls the speed, so they can't go faster than the **speed limit**.

B This monorail in New Zealand is a new solution for commuters in a **traffic jam** during **rush hour**. The passenger sits in a pod and can cycle over people's heads. Google has already invested over $1 million in this idea.

C In the future, the Hyperloop could be a common type of public transportation. It's a long tube with no air inside, and passengers sit inside pods that travel at 1,200 kilometers per hour. It would reduce air and noise pollution. There are already plans for the first Hyperloop between **downtown** San Francisco and Los Angeles. The distance is around 600 kilometers, and it would only take 30 minutes of travel time.

Grammar comparatives and superlatives

5 ▶19 Work in pairs. Listen to a conversation between two colleagues at work. Which types of transportation do they talk about? What advantages and disadvantages do they mention?

6 ▶19 Look at the grammar box below and circle the correct options in these sentences. Listen again and check.

1 Eight-thirty in the morning is the *bad / worst* time for traffic.
2 My bicycle is *faster / fastest* than your car during rush hour!
3 I travel *far / farther* than you.
4 They're better, but they're also *more / most* expensive.
5 The *most fast / fastest* bus takes over an hour.

▶ COMPARATIVES and SUPERLATIVES		
Regular adjectives	**Comparative**	**Superlative**
fast	*faster*	*fastest*
big	*bigger*	*biggest*
expensive	*more expensive*	*most expensive*
Irregular adjectives		
far	*farther*	*farthest*
good	*better*	*best*
bad	*worse*	*worst*

For more information and practice, see page 160.

7 Work in pairs. Look at the grammar box. Answer these questions.

1 What letters do we add to short adjectives (*fast, cheap*, etc.) to form comparative and superlative adjectives?
2 We use *more* before longer adjectives to make the comparative. What word do we use to make the superlative?
3 Which word often comes after a comparative adjective? Which word normally comes before a superlative adjective?

8 Pronunciation *than*

a ▶20 Listen to the pronunciation of *than* in these sentences. Listen again and repeat.

1 Cars are faster than bicycles.
2 Bicycles are better for the environment than cars.

b Work in pairs. Practice saying these sentences.

1 I travel farther than you.
2 A train is more expensive than a bus.

9 Complete this report about a transportation survey. Write the correct comparative or superlative form of the adjectives in parentheses.

Report on local transportation

For commuting and daytime travel in our town, the [1] _____ (popular) form of transportation is the bus because it's [2] _____ (cheap) than going by car or taxi. However, some people in the survey prefer to cycle because the bus is [3] _____ (slow) than a bicycle during rush hour. Everyone said that parking downtown is the [4] _____ (big) problem, so people don't often use their cars. As a result, taxis are [5] _____ (popular) than private cars.

Speaking *my* **Life**

10 Work in pairs. Form comparative and superlative sentences with these transportation words and adjectives. How many sentences can you make in three minutes?

trains	cars		fast	cheap	bad
taxis	buses		slow	popular	
planes	ships		expensive	safe	
bicycles	motorcycles		quick	good	

*Trains are **quicker than** cars, but planes are **the fastest** type of transportation.*

11 Work in pairs. Find out about your partner's commute to work or school. Take turns asking and answering these questions.

1 How far do you travel to work or school?
2 What type of transportation do you use?
3 How long does it take?
4 How much does it cost every week?

12 With your partner, form sentences comparing your commutes.

*My home is **farther** from school **than** yours. / Your home is **closer than** mine.*

13 Work with another pair. Compare your information. Find out:

1 who lives the closest to / farthest away from work or school
   *Mario lives **the closest to** work, and Ahmed lives **the farthest away.***
2 who has the shortest / longest commute
3 who has the cheapest / most expensive commute each week
4 which type of transportation is the least / most popular in the group

3b Transportation around the world

Listening

1 Work in pairs. Look at the photos. Where do you think they were taken? What are the advantages of using animals for transportation in these places?

2 ▶ 21 Work in pairs. Listen to a documentary about animal transportation. Why does the speaker say camels and huskies are better than cars?

3 ▶ 21 Listen to the documentary again. What do these numbers describe? Make notes and compare your answers with a partner.

Camels	Huskies
50 degrees	-50 degrees
40 kilometers	6 and 8 huskies
3 to 5 days	1,600 kilometers

Grammar *as … as*

> ▶ **AS … AS**
>
> 1 *In some parts of the world, animal transportation is **as** popular **as** these modern vehicles.*
> 2 *In winter, northern Alaska can be **as** cold **as** the North Pole.*
> 3 *For long distances, modern vehicles are **not as** good **as** camels.*
> 4 *A camel isn't **as** comfortable **as** a car.*
>
> For more information and practice, see page 160.

4 Work in pairs. Look at the grammar box and answer these questions.

    a Which two sentences say two things are the same or equal?
    b Which two sentences say two things are different, and one thing is less than the other?

5 Work in pairs and rewrite these sentences. Use *as … as* or *not as … as* and the adjective in parentheses.

    1 The subway from Hong Kong airport to Kowloon costs $100, and a taxi costs $210. (not / expensive)
       The subway from Hong Kong airport to Kowloon isn't as expensive as a taxi.
    2 The ferry from Jordan to Egypt takes one hour. A bus ride over land takes two hours. (not / slow)
    3 During rush hour in New York, riding a bike to work and taking a bus take the same amount of time. (fast)
    4 In Colombia and Greece, 9% of households own motorcycles. (popular)

6 Pronunciation sentence stress

▶ 22 Listen to these sentences. Underline the stressed word in each sentence. Then listen again and repeat.

1 Riding a bike is as popular as jogging.
2 Trains aren't as expensive as taxis.
3 Los Angeles airport is as busy as London Heathrow.
4 A car isn't as fast as a bicycle in a traffic jam.

7 Work in pairs. Ask questions to find out how similar or different you and your partner are. Then write sentences.

Carlos is as tall as me. / He isn't as old as me.

His family isn't as big as mine.

Vocabulary transportation adjectives

8 Read part of a news article about taxis in London. What does it compare?

BATTLE OF THE TAXIS

When you travel in London, the city's famous black taxis or black cabs are a **convenient** type of transportation. On any main road, there are plenty of cabs, and even with four or five people, they're **comfortable** to ride in. But now the **traditional** black cab has competition from private taxis such as Addison Lee. Using your cell phone, you can book a private taxi for a certain time—they are very **punctual**. Sometimes these private taxis are also a bit cheaper and a little faster. However, in bad traffic, black-cab drivers say their cabs are much faster. They have to learn all the roads around London, so they don't use GPS, and they know the best routes around the city. They think that private taxis are a lot less **reliable** in rush-hour traffic.

9 Find the words in **bold** in the article. Then match them with their definitions (1–5).

1 It's always on time. _____
2 It has existed for a long time. _____
3 It's nice to sit in. _____
4 It's nearby or easy to use. _____
5 It does what you need it to. _____

Grammar comparative modifiers

▶ **COMPARATIVE MODIFIERS**

Sometimes these private taxis are **a bit** cheaper and **a little** faster.
Black-cab drivers are **much** faster because they know the best routes.
They think that private taxis are **a lot** less reliable.

For more information and practice, see page 160.

10 Look at the grammar box. Complete these rules (1–2) with the comparative modifiers in **bold** in the grammar box.

1 To talk about a small difference, we use _____ or _____ before a comparative adjective.
2 To talk about a big difference, we use _____ or _____ before a comparative adjective.

11 Work in pairs. Look at the information about transportation for visitors to Tokyo. Form sentences using these ideas and comparative modifiers.

1 A taxi is / expensive than …
   *Taking a taxi is **a lot more** expensive than taking a bus.*
2 The subway is / frequent than …
3 Taxis are / quick than …

	Subway Train	Taxi	Bus
Prices	¥800 for unlimited use of all subway lines for 24 hours	Around ¥300 for every kilometer traveled	¥500 for unlimited travel anywhere in the main areas of the city for one day
Frequency	About every 3 minutes during peak hours	All the time at taxi stands and on busy streets	A bus comes about every 5 minutes
Other information	13 subway lines cover every part of Tokyo	Red shows the taxi is vacant; a green plate means it's occupied	Buses are slower than taxis and subways; buses don't run at night

Speaking ▐my▐Life▐

12 What advice would you give a visitor arriving in your country for the first time? What are the best ways to get around? Tell your partner.

3c The end of the road

Reading

1 You are going to read an article about a city in India. Write one thing you know about India. Then tell the class.

2 Read the article. Which paragraph (1–3) talks about:

  a why people like rickshaws in Kolkata? ____
  b modern transportation in Kolkata? ____
  c the end of the old rickshaws in Kolkata? ____

3 Work in pairs. Read the article again and answer these questions.

  1 What is the population of Kolkata?
  2 What are streets like in Kolkata?
  3 Where is it safer for pedestrians to walk? Why?
  4 Why do local housewives and tourists like taking rickshaws?
  5 Some politicians want a new type of rickshaw. How is it different?
  6 How many people pull the old rickshaws in Kolkata?
  7 Why don't these drivers use the new rickshaws?

Vocabulary transportation verbs

4 Read paragraphs 1 and 2 of the article again. Find verbs or verb phrases that can replace the verbs in **bold** below.

  1 I'd prefer to **travel by** taxi to the airport. It's much quicker.
     g*o*___ b*y*___

  2 I can **collect** the children from school on my way home from work.
     p___ u___

  3 I need to go now if I want to **get** the next train.
     c___

  4 You'd better leave now or you will **not make** your flight.
     m___

  5 Tell the driver to **leave you** outside the restaurant.
     d___ you o___

Critical thinking opinions for and against

5 Work in pairs. There are five different groups of people mentioned in the article: shoppers, tourists, politicians, children (and parents), and rickshaw drivers. Which groups:

  1 are for hand-pulled rickshaws in Kolkata?
  2 are against the hand-pulled rickshaws?

  Give reasons for your answers.

6 Work in pairs. Do you think the writer gives a balanced view of the opinions on both sides? Why or why not?

Speaking

7 Look at the photo above of a pedicab. Then work in groups. You want to start a pedicab company in your town or city. Discuss these questions and make notes.

  1 Who are your main customers? (commuters, tourists, etc.)
  2 Why are pedicabs better than other types of transportation (buses, taxis, etc.)?
  3 How much do you charge? Are you cheaper or more expensive than other transportation?
  4 What is the name of your business? How can you advertise your business? (on the internet, on TV, etc.)

8 As a group, give a presentation about your pedicab company to the class. Listen to other groups and compare your ideas. Which group has the best ideas?

The end
of the
road

▶ 23

1 Kolkata is the capital of West Bengal in India. It has a population of around 15 million people,
5 and rush hour starts early in the morning. All day there are traffic jams with cars, public buses, taxis, motorcycles, and pedicabs,[1] and drivers honk
10 their horns[2] from morning to night. You can also catch the train or get on the subway, but those are busy, too. For pedestrians, Kolkata can be
15 dangerous—crossing the road is especially difficult. Fortunately, the old parts of the city have smaller streets that are better for pedestrians. Cars can't drive
20 down them, so they are much quieter and a lot safer.

2 In these old streets, you'll see men pulling rickshaws. Rickshaws are a traditional type of transportation in the city, and local people still like using them. In the morning, the drivers pick
25 up children and take them to school. And if you miss your bus to work, a hand-pulled rickshaw is much cheaper than taking a taxi. Later on in the day, housewives often prefer to go by rickshaw to the local markets. The drivers drop the women off with their shopping outside their houses; no other type of public
30 transportation can do that! So rickshaws are popular with many local people. When the traffic is very bad, you can go anywhere by rickshaw. Kolkata is one of the last cities in the world with hand-pulled rickshaws, so the drivers also make money from tourists. Visitors to the city often want to get a photograph of themselves
35 sitting on a rickshaw because it's a famous symbol of Kolkata.

3 However, not everyone thinks the famous rickshaws are a good idea. Some local politicians don't like this old type of transportation because they think it's wrong for one human to pull another. Instead, they want more rickshaw drivers to
40 use pedicabs or modern electric rickshaws, which are clean and fast. The problem is that Kolkata has around 2,000 traditional rickshaw drivers. They are often men from villages in the countryside, and they don't have any other job. The new electric rickshaws are very expensive, so these drivers can't afford
45 them. For these men, it's probably the end of the road for the traditional rickshaw and their way of life.

[1] **pedicab** (n) /ˈpedɪkæb/ a type of taxi with no engine. The driver pedals.
[2] **honk your horn** (exp) /hɒŋk jɔː hɔːrn/ make a loud noise in a car to tell people you are there

3d Getting around town

Vocabulary taking transportation

1 Look at these pairs of words (1–5). Match the words with their definitions (a or b).

1 stop _b_ / stand _a_
   a the place you get a taxi
   b the place you get a bus
2 fare ___ / price ___
   a the money you pay for a trip by bus, train, or taxi
   b the amount of money something costs
3 change ___ / receipt ___
   a the money you get back when you pay more than the price
   b the piece of paper you receive to show you paid for something
4 gate ___ / platform ___
   a the place you get on a train
   b the place you get on a plane
5 book ___ / check in ___
   a when you buy a ticket in advance
   b when you arrive at an airport and register for a flight

Real life going on a trip

2 ▶ 24 Work in pairs. Listen to five conversations. Javier and Shelley are going to the airport, but they take different transportation. Answer the questions.

1 Where does Javier ask the taxi driver to take him?
2 How much is the taxi fare?
3 Where does Shelley want to go?
4 How much is Javier's train ticket? Which platform does the train leave from?
5 What does Shelley show the woman? How many bags does she check in?

3 ▶ 24 Look at the expressions for going on a trip. Then listen to the conversations again. Circle the sentences you hear.

> ▶ **GOING ON A TRIP**
>
> **In a taxi**
> I'd like to go to the station, please.
> You can stop here.
> How much is that?
> Do you have change?
> Do you want a receipt?
>
> **On a bus**
> Do you stop at the airport?
> A one-way or round-trip ticket?
> Please stop at the next one.
> That's two dollars.
>
> **At the train station**
> A round-trip ticket to the airport, please.
> First or second class?
> One way or round trip?
> Which platform is it?
>
> **At the airport**
> Can I see your passport?
> How many bags are you checking in?
> I only have this carry-on.
> Window or aisle seat?
> Can I get a seat next to my friend?

4 Pronunciation intonation

▶ 25 In everyday English, people don't always use full questions. For example, they can say *One way or round trip?* instead of *Do you want a one-way or round-trip ticket?* Listen to these questions. Mark the intonation ➚ or ➘.

1 One way or round trip?
2 Window or aisle seat?
3 Credit card or cash?
4 Bus or train?
5 North or south?
6 First or second class?

5 Work in pairs. Look at the four situations (a–d) with people going to an airport. Act out conversations using the expressions for going on a trip to help you.

Student A: You are the passenger.

Student B: Take the other role in the conversations (e.g., the taxi driver).

Then change roles and repeat.

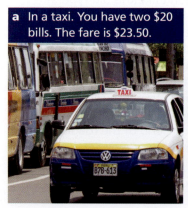

a In a taxi. You have two $20 bills. The fare is $23.50.

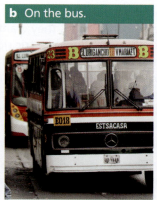

b On the bus.

c At the train station.

d At the airport. You have two bags.

3e Quick communication

Writing notes and messages

1 Work in pairs. How do you normally send notes and messages to friends and colleagues? By text or email? What other ways do you use?

2 Read the notes and messages (1–8). Match them with the reasons for writing (a–e).

a thanking
b apologizing
c giving travel information
d suggesting a time and place to meet
e giving a message from someone else

3 Writing skill writing in note form

a Work in pairs. People often leave out words in notes and messages. Look again at the notes and messages in Exercise 2. Find places where the writers have left out these kinds of words.

- articles (e.g., *a, the*)
- pronouns (e.g., *I, me*)
- auxiliary verbs (e.g., *do, are*)
- polite forms (e.g., *Would you like to …? Can we …?*)

(Can we) Meet outside (the) airport at 2? (Is that) OK?

b How would you rewrite these phone messages as shorter text messages? Discuss with a partner.

1 "I'm sorry, but I'm stuck in a traffic jam. I'll see you in half an hour."
Sorry. Stuck in traffic. See you in 30 mins.
2 "Thank you for booking the train tickets. I'll pay you when we meet at the station."
3 "My flight is an hour late. Meet me in the arrivals area at five o'clock."

4 Work in pairs. Write a short note or message for each situation (1–3).

1 You have to work late. Write a text to your friend. Say you will arrive at the restaurant an hour later.
2 You are meeting a friend downtown tonight. Ask your friend to meet you at the taxi stand outside the train station.
3 You cannot travel with your friend on the subway to the airport. Explain that you will take the bus and meet him or her in the check-in area.

5 Think of another situation on your own and write a short message to your partner. Then exchange messages. Can you understand the other person's message? Write a reply if necessary.

1

Meet outside airport at 2? OK?

2

Sorry. Bus late. Will be 15 minutes late.

3

Javier called. Call him back. 213-509-6995.

4

Train leaves platform 6.

5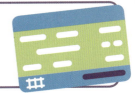

Thanks for getting tickets. Here's the money.

6

Plane at gate 6.

7

Am in taxi. See you outside in 5?

8

Afraid I was late, so missed meeting. My apologies.

3f Indian Railways

At the Victoria Terminus in Mumbai, India, it always seems to be rush hour.

Before you watch

1 Work in pairs. Look at the photo and the caption. Why do you think trains are a popular type of transportation in India?

2 Key vocabulary

a Work in pairs. Read the sentences (1–5). The words in **bold** are used in the video. Guess the meaning of these words.

1 Don't walk on the railway **track**! A train might come.
2 Some of the trains in India have **impressive** names like *The Himalayan Queen*.
3 I live in a **rural** village about thirty kilometers from the nearest town.
4 This toy train is a **miniature** of the real thing.
5 My company has a large **workforce**. We employ over five hundred people.

b Write the words in **bold** in Exercise 2a next to their definitions (a–e).

a important-sounding _____
b the metal line that a train runs on _____
c the group of people who work for a company _____
d in the countryside _____
e a small copy or model _____

While you watch

3 ▶ **3.1** Watch the video about Indian Railways with the sound OFF. Number these actions in the order you see them (1–6).

____ A man is checking the railway track with a hammer.
____ A train is traveling in the Indian countryside.
_1_ Hundreds of people are walking on a platform during rush hour.
____ People are playing a game on the train.
____ A man with a white beard is dancing with two swords.
____ A man is serving food on the train.

4 ▶ **3.1** Watch the video with the sound ON. Circle the correct options.

1 Every day, approximately *two hundred thousand / two million* passengers pass through the Victoria Terminus in Mumbai.
2 There are over *one billion / two billion* people in India.
3 The British built the railways in India in the *eighteenth / nineteenth* century.
4 The first steam train in India was in eighteen *thirty-three / fifty-three*.
5 There are over *thirty-eight thousand / three thousand eight hundred* miles of railway track in India.

6 The Grand Trunk Express has traveled through India since nineteen *twenty-nine / thirty-nine*.
7 India's railways carry *four million / four billion* passengers every year.
8 Indian Railways employs *fifty thousand / one and a half million* staff.

After you watch

5 Vocabulary in context

a ▶ **3.2** Watch the clips from the video. Choose the correct meaning of the words and phrases.

b Work in pairs. Ask and answer these questions.

1 Does your country have an enormous public transportation system? Is the transportation system in your country in good condition? Why or why not?
2 What everyday situations do you find most stressful? Why?
3 In your country, which company is one of the largest employers? What do they make or provide?

6 ▶ **3.3** You are going to prepare a narration for a new version of the Indian Railways video. It's called *A one-minute journey on the Indian Railways*. As you watch, take notes about what you see in each part.

• Rush hour in Mumbai (0:00–0:15)
• On the train (0:16–0:38)
• The workforce (0:39–0:50)
• At the station (0:51–1:00)

7 Now write a script for the new video. Describe what you can see in the video and add any important facts and figures about Indian Railways. Use some of these words and phrases.

checking the track	playing games
cities and rural villages	rush hour
enormous	station
good condition	stressful
passengers	platform
workforce	dancing

8 Work with a partner. Your teacher will play the new video twice. As you watch, take turns reading your script and narrating the video.

UNIT 3 REVIEW AND MEMORY BOOSTER

Grammar

1 Complete the article with the correct form of the adjectives in parentheses.

Santiago is the ¹ _____ (large) city in Chile, with a population of five million people. It has some of the ² _____ (beautiful) buildings in the world, but in the past, it was the ³ _____ (polluted) city in Chile. Its streets weren't as ⁴ _____ (clean) as they are today. Nowadays, public transportation around the city is also much ⁵ _____ (good), and the city center isn't as ⁶ _____ (noisy). Riding bikes is also a lot ⁷ _____ (popular) these days because there are new bike paths and people can use electric bikes.

2 **>> MB** Work in pairs. Form three sentences comparing your town or city to Santiago. Talk about:

- size and population
- buildings and streets
- traffic and public transportation

I CAN
use comparative and superlative adjectives
use *as … as*

Vocabulary

3 Match words from A with words from B to make compound nouns. Then complete the sentences with the compound nouns.

A	traffic	rush	bus	speed

B	hour	stop	limit	jam

1 There's a _____ _____ on the highway. Nothing's moving.
2 _____ _____ starts at about seven in the morning.
3 Wait at the _____ _____ . Another bus should arrive in ten minutes.
4 Slow down! The _____ _____ is only 30 kilometers an hour on this road.

4 Which words can follow the words in **bold**? Cross out the incorrect word or words.

1 **go by** bus, feet, plane, bicycle
2 **go on** a taxi, a ship, foot, a ferry
3 **catch** a train, a plane, a truck, a bus
4 **drop off** your shopping, your children, the subway

5 **>> MB** Work in pairs. Look at the forms of transportation and answer the questions (1–7). Give reasons for your answers.

taxi	rickshaw	camel
bus	airplane	train

1 Which types of transportation are slow but reliable?
2 Which are comfortable and convenient?
3 Which is the cheapest?
4 Which goes the farthest in a short time?
5 Which lands at a gate?
6 Which stops at a stand?
7 Which are good for sightseeing in a city?

I CAN
talk about transportation

Real life

6 Complete the conversation at a train station with the words and phrases in the box.

platform	ticket	one way
round trip	receipt	

A: I'd like a train ¹ _____ to Boston.
B: ² _____ or round trip?
A: ³ _____ , please.
B: That's twenty-one dollars and fifty cents. Do you want a ⁴ _____ ?
A: Yes, please. Which ⁵ _____ is it?
B: Three.

7 **>> MB** Work in pairs. Write a similar conversation between two people at an airport. Use these phrases.

see your passport	check in
a carry-on	window or aisle

I CAN
buy tickets and use different types of transportation

Unit 4 Challenges

Rumbling Falls Cave, Tennessee

FEATURES

46 Adventurers of the year

Profiles of some of the world's top adventurers

48 An impossible decision

The real-life story of two climbers and a difficult decision

50 Challenge yourself

Find out about some challenges for the mind

54 A microadventure

A video about two friends who spend 24 hours in Croatia

1 Work in pairs. Look at the photo. Where is the man? Do you think this activity looks exciting or dangerous? Would you like to do this?

2 ▶ 26 Work in pairs. Listen to a caver talking about his hobby. Answer the questions.

1 Why do his co-workers think he is "a little crazy"?
2 Why do cavers work in teams?
3 How do you get to Rumbling Falls Cave?

3 Look at these sentences from Vic's description. Match the words in **bold** (1–3) with their definitions (a–c).

1 Sometimes you have to **take a risk** when you go caving.
2 Every cave gives you a different **challenge**.
3 Getting to Rumbling Falls Cave is probably my biggest **achievement** as a caver so far.

a do something that can be dangerous _____
b success in something after a lot of hard work and effort (e.g., passing an examination) _____
c something very difficult to do _____

4 Work in groups. Discuss these questions.

1 Are you a person who takes risks or are you usually very careful?
2 What is a big achievement in your life so far?
3 What will be a big challenge for you in the future?

45

4a Adventurers of the year

Reading

1 Read the article. Are these sentences about Pasang, Marjan, or both of them? Write 1–6 in the diagram.

1. She was born in Nepal.
2. Her father helped her.
3. She started when she was a teenager.
4. She trained for her job.
5. She competed in other countries.
6. She changed other people's lives.

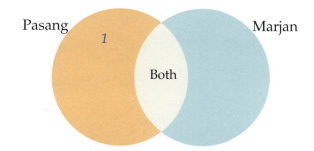

Pasang

Marjan

1

Both

2 Read the article again. Work in pairs and discuss the questions.

1. What do you think was Pasang's biggest challenge?
2. Why is she famous?
3. What was Marjan's ambition?
4. What were her team's achievements?

Grammar simple past

> **SIMPLE PAST**

We use the simple past to talk about finished actions, events, or situations in the past.
Pasang Lhamu Sherpa Akita **lived** with her younger sister in Lukla.
Marjan Sadequi **grew up** in the capital city of Kabul.
People **didn't have** homes or food.
It **wasn't** easy to practice on the roads of Kabul.

For more information and practice, see page 162.

▶ 27

ADVENTURERS *of the* YEAR

EVERY YEAR, READERS OF *NATIONAL GEOGRAPHIC* MAGAZINE VOTE FOR THEIR ADVENTURERS OF THE YEAR. HERE ARE TWO OF THEM.

THE MOUNTAINEER

As a child, Pasang Lhamu Sherpa Akita lived with her younger sister in Lukla, a town in northeastern Nepal. Pasang's parents died when she was young. As a teenager, she trained as a mountaineer. She worked as a mountain guide, and she climbed Mount Everest when she was only 22. In 2015, there was a terrible earthquake in Nepal. Many people didn't have homes or food, so Pasang helped them. These days, she also works to improve education in Nepal, and is famous for her volunteer work as well as her mountaineering.

THE CYCLIST

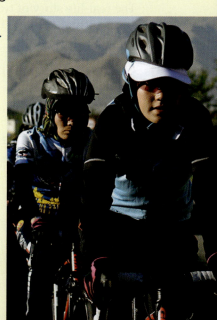

Marjan Sadequi was born in Afghanistan and grew up in the capital city of Kabul. Her father was the national cycling coach for the men's team, and from very early on in life, Marjan's ambition was to become a cyclist. Her father gave Marjan her first bicycle when she was a teenager, and he soon saw how much Marjan loved cycling. As a result, he formed a new women's cycling team with his daughter and ten other women. It wasn't easy to practice on the roads of Kabul, but in 2013, the team went to New Delhi and they had their first international competition against other women's cycling teams. They didn't win, but they entered more races in Pakistan, Kazakhstan, and South Korea. Because of Marjan and her team's achievements, more women are now cycling in Afghanistan.

3 Look at the grammar box on page 46. Then underline the verbs in the past tense in *Adventurers of the Year*. Which are regular? Which are irregular?

4 Work in pairs. Answer these questions.

1 What do we add to regular verbs to form the simple past? What do we add if the verb ends in *-e*? What if the verb ends in *-y*?
2 What is the base form of the irregular verbs you underlined?
   grew up—grow up
3 How do we form the negative of most simple past verbs? How do we form the negative of *be*?

5 Pronunciation /d/, /t/, or /ɪd/

▶ **28** Listen to the *-ed* ending of these regular verbs. Is the sound /d/, /t/, or /ɪd/? Circle your answers. Then listen again and repeat.

1 lived   /d/ /t/ /ɪd/   5 waited   /d/ /t/ /ɪd/
2 finished   /d/ /t/ /ɪd/   6 looked   /d/ /t/ /ɪd/
3 wanted   /d/ /t/ /ɪd/   7 decided /d/ /t/ /ɪd/
4 studied   /d/ /t/ /ɪd/   8 climbed /d/ /t/ /ɪd/

6 Complete the text about another adventurer. Use the simple past form of the verbs in parentheses.

THE PHOTOGRAPHER

Reza ¹ _____was_____ (be) born in Tabriz, Iran, in 1952. He ² _____ (study) architecture at a college in Tehran, but he ³ _____ (not / become) an architect. When he was a teenager, Reza ⁴ _____ (love) photography, and after college, he ⁵ _____ (get) a job with a local newspaper as a photographer. But he ⁶ _____ (not / want) to take photos of local news, so in 1978 he ⁷ _____ (go) abroad and he ⁸ _____ (take) photos of wars. These days, he works for *National Geographic* magazine.

7 Read the text about Reza again. Work in pairs. Answer the questions.

1 When was Reza born?
2 Where did he study architecture?
3 What did he love when he was a teenager?
4 What did he do after college?
5 Did he want to take photos of local news?
6 When did he go abroad?

▶ **SIMPLE PAST QUESTIONS**

*When **was** Reza born?*
*Where **did** he **study** architecture?*
***Did** he **want** to take photos of local news?*

For more information and practice, see page 162.

8 Look at the grammar box above. Circle the correct option (a or b) to complete these rules.

1 With most regular and irregular verbs, we make questions with _____ .
   a the simple past form of the verb
   b *did* + base form of the verb
2 With *be*, we make questions with _____ .
   a *was* and *were*
   b *did* + base form of the verb

9 Read these questions and answers from interviews with Pasang and Marjan. Complete the questions.

1 I: Where _did you live_ as a child?
   P: In Lukla, in northeastern Nepal.
2 I: When _____ Mount Everest?
   P: When I was 22 years old.
3 I: Who _____ after the earthquake?
   P: People with no homes and no food.
4 I: _____ you born?
   M: In Afghanistan.
5 I: _____ your first international race?
   M: No, we didn't.

Speaking [my Life]

10 Write six questions to ask your partner about the past. Use some of these ideas.

where / born?   where / grow up?
when / learn / to ride a bike?
when / start / studying English?
where / go / vacation / last year?
go / abroad / last year?   go / college?
what / be / first job?

11 Work in pairs. Take turns interviewing each other. Make notes about your partner's answers.

12 Work with a new partner. Describe your first partner's life from Exercise 11.

4b An impossible decision

Vocabulary
personal qualities

1 Work in groups. Read this English expression and discuss the questions.

"Two heads are better than one."

1 What do you think the expression means?
2 Do you have a similar expression in your language?
3 What are the advantages and disadvantages of working in teams?
4 What do you think makes a good team member?

2 Read the sentences about what makes a good team member. Write the adjectives in the box next to the matching sentence.

experienced	friendly	hardworking
kind	patient	positive

A good team member:
1 likes meeting people and gets along with everyone. _____*friendly*_____
2 is a good listener and thinks about other people. _____
3 gives people the time they need and waits for them. _____
4 is always happy and looks for the good things in life. _____
5 works extra hours when it's necessary. _____
6 knows a lot about his or her area of work. _____

3 Work in pairs. Which qualities in Exercise 2 do these people need? Why?

a close friend	a teacher	a language learner
a manager	a parent	a president

A good teacher is patient because the students need time to learn.

Listening

4 What difficult decisions do people have to make in life? What decisions do you have to make at work or for your studies? Tell your partner.

I left my old company last year. It was difficult because I had a lot of good colleagues there. But I wanted a new challenge.

5 ▶ 29 Listen to the first part of a true story about two climbers named Joe Simpson and Simon Yates. Number these pictures (a–d) in the correct order (1–4).

6 Work in pairs. What was Yates's impossible decision at the end? What do you think he did?

7 ▶ 30 Now listen to the whole story. Work in pairs and answer the questions.

1 What two personal qualities from Exercise 2 did Simpson and Yates have?
2 Why didn't they stay at the top of the mountain for very long?
3 What decision did Yates make in the end?
4 The next day, what did Yates think about Simpson?
5 What did Yates hear in the night?
6 How did the story of Yates and Simpson become famous?

Grammar past continuous and simple past

> **PAST CONTINUOUS and SIMPLE PAST**
>
> *While they **were going** down the mountain, Simpson **fell**. He **wasn't moving**, but he **was** still **breathing**.*
> Note: We often use *when* and *while* to talk about one action happening at the same time as another.
>
> For more information and practice, see page 162.

8 Look at the sentences in the grammar box. Work in pairs and answer these questions.

1 Which verb talks about a completed action?
2 Which verbs talk about actions in progress at a moment in the past?
3 We often use the two verb forms together. Which verb form is used for the longer, continuing activity? Which form is used for the shorter, finished action?
4 What is the auxiliary verb in the past continuous? What is the form of the main verb?

9 The sentences below describe the story of Simpson and Yates. Circle the correct options to complete the sentences.

1 The sun *shone* /(*was shining*) when Simpson and Yates left their tents on the first day.
2 When they reached the top of the mountain, it *snowed* / *was snowing*.
3 While they were going down the mountain, Simpson *broke* / *was breaking* his knee.
4 For an hour, Yates held the rope, but it *pulled* / *was pulling* him off the mountain.
5 Yates was sleeping in his tent, but he suddenly *woke up* / *was waking up*.
6 Finally, Yates *found* / *was finding* Simpson on the ground.

10 Complete each sentence with one verb in the past continuous form and one verb in the simple past form.

1 I _____*was working*_____ (work) on my own when a group of people _____*came*_____ (come) into my office.
2 We _____ (meet) them when they _____ (live) above our apartment.
3 They _____ (not get along) very well, so the team _____ (agree) to have a meeting.
4 The weather _____ (be) cold this morning, but it _____ (not rain).
5 I saw you across the street, but I _____ (not stop) because I _____ (run) to my job interview!
6 What _____ he _____ (do) when you _____ (call) him?
7 Which cities _____ they _____ (visit) while they _____ (travel)?
8 Why _____ you _____ (answer) that call while we _____ (watch) the movie?

11 Pronunciation *was / were*

a ▶ 31 Work in pairs. Listen to sentences 1 to 4 from Exercise 10. Notice the pronunciation of *was, were, wasn't,* and *weren't*. Which are stressed and which are unstressed?

b ▶ 31 Listen again and repeat the sentences.

Speaking myLife

12 Which of these events happened to you in the past? Write some sentences about them and state when the events happened.

> broke a bone
> achieved something with a team of other people
> got a first job
> had an accident
> had an argument with a close friend
> received really good news
> was late for an important meeting

I broke my arm on my sixth birthday.

13 Work in pairs. Tell your partner about the things that happened to you. Take turns asking and answering questions about what you were doing when the events happened.

A: *I **broke** my arm on my sixth birthday.*
B: *What **were** you **doing** when it happened?*
A: *I **was riding** my first bicycle when I **fell off**.*

4c Challenge yourself

Reading

1 Work in pairs. Answer this riddle and solve the matchstick puzzle. Then take the numbers memory challenge on page 51. Turn to page 155 to find the answers.

A riddle: *What is yours, but other people use it more than you?*

A puzzle: **Move two matchsticks and make four equal squares.**

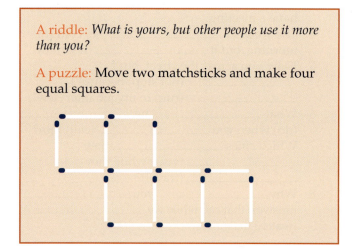

2 Work in pairs. Why do you think people like doing these types of challenges?

3 Read the article on page 51. Are these sentences true (T) or false (F)?

1 Professor Rubik taught students about architecture.	T	F
2 He made the cube to teach his students about puzzles.	T	F
3 Professor Rubik solved the cube right away.	T	F
4 A robot can solve a Rubik's cube faster than a human.	T	F
5 Some scientists think puzzles are good for older people's brains.	T	F
6 A study showed that playing video games has no impact on human memory.	T	F

Critical thinking
looking for evidence

4 *Evidence* is factual information to support an idea. Check (✓) the three types of evidence the writer uses in the article. Which does he not use?

- ☐ facts from history
- ☐ data (e.g., numbers and amounts)
- ☐ quotes from people
- ☐ results from a scientific study

5 Read these ideas (a–c) from the article and answer the questions (1–2).

a The Rubik's cube became one of the most popular toys in history.
b Our brain naturally loves solving problems.
c Some scientists think puzzles and games can improve memory in the elderly.

1 Which two ideas have evidence in the article to support them? Underline this evidence. ____
2 Which idea doesn't have much evidence in the article? (It's the writer's opinion.) ____

Wordbuilding **verbs and nouns**

> **WORDBUILDING verbs and nouns**
>
> Some words have a verb form and a noun form. Sometimes the verb and noun form is the same:
> *challenge* (v), *challenge* (n)
> Sometimes the forms are different:
> *achieve* (v), *achievement* (n)
>
> For more practice, see Workbook page 35.

6 Look at the wordbuilding box below. Complete this chart with words from the article.

Verb	Noun
challenge	challenge
achieve	achievement
1 _____	solution
2 _____	player
3 _____	improvement
memorize	4 _____
test	5 _____
6 _____	score

Writing and speaking

7 Work in pairs. Use the words in Exercise 6 to write a list of tips for someone who is a beginner in English. Take turns giving your partner advice about the best ways to learn.

When you study for a test, you should memorize ...

CHALLENGE YOURSELF

THE NUMBERS MEMORY CHALLENGE

Cover the groups of numbers in this list. Then look at the first group (on the top line), cover it again, and try to say the numbers. Then look at the second group of numbers (on the second line), cover them, and try to say them.

Continue down the list. When do you stop remembering all the numbers in a group?

```
4 9 2 6
5 7 8 4 3
9 5 3 4 5 6
7 4 3 0 6 7 3
8 9 3 1 4 2 8 9
6 3 9 8 1 8 5 3 1
9 2 7 8 3 6 9 7 0 8
```

▶ 32

1   In 1974, Professor Erno Rubik was looking for an interesting way to teach his architecture students about 3D[1] geometry.[2] To do this, he made a cube with nine other cubes on each of its sides. The smaller cubes were different colors, and you could turn them in different directions. The challenge was to make each side all one color. The problem was that there
5   are 43 quintillion (43,000,000,000,000,000,000) ways to move the cubes. As a result, it took Professor Rubik over a month to solve his own problem.

2   In the end, the Rubik's cube became one of the most popular toys in history. Over 400 million Rubik's cubes have been sold around the world, and one in seven people have played with one. In 2016, a Dutch man named Mats Valk solved the Rubik's cube in 4.74 seconds—
10   the world record for a human at the time. A robot beat him with a time of 1.019 seconds.

3   So why do humans love challenging themselves with puzzles like the Rubik's cube? It's the same reason we like crosswords and puzzles in newspapers, or why we play games on our cell phones. Our brain naturally loves solving problems.

4   Some scientists also think puzzles and games can improve
15   memory in the elderly. In one study at Illinois University, the researchers studied how video games help older people's mental health. In their study, twenty adults over the age of sixty played a video game for a long period, while
20   another twenty adults over sixty did not. Afterwards, they gave all forty adults a test of memory and mental skill. Overall, the video game players scored higher on the test, which
25   means a challenging video game could be good for our brains.

---

[1] **3D** (adj) /ˌθriːˈdiː/ three-dimensional
[2] **geometry** (n) /dʒiːˈɒmətri/ mathematical subject about shapes and sizes

4d True stories

Real life telling a story

1 ▶ 33 Listen to two friends talking about a camping trip. Work in pairs and answer the questions.

1 Was the start of the weekend good or bad?
2 What happened to the car?
3 Who helped them?
4 What was the problem when they found the campsite?
5 Where did they go instead?

2 ▶ 33 Listen again. Complete the conversation with the words you hear.

A: Hi, Mark. How was your camping trip?
B: It was great in the end, but we had a terrible time at the beginning.
A: Why?
B: ¹_____ , we left the house late, and then after only half an hour, the car broke down.
A: Oh, no! ²_____ ?
B: ³_____ , there was a garage nearby and the mechanic fixed the problem. But ⁴_____ we arrived at the forest, it was getting dark. ⁵_____ we drove around for about an hour, we ⁶_____ found the campsite, but it was completely dark by then. And it was raining!
A: Really? So ⁷_____ ?
B: We found a nice, warm hotel down the road!
A: That was lucky!
B: Yes, it was a great hotel. ⁸_____ , we stayed there for the whole weekend.
A: ⁹_____ !

3 Look at the expressions for telling a story. Match the expressions in Exercise 2 (1–9) with the headings (a–d).

> ▶ **TELLING A STORY**
>
> **a Sequencing the story** *1,*_____
> At the beginning, … Then … Next, … While …
>
> **b Introducing good and bad news** _____
> Luckily, … But … Unfortunately, …
>
> **c Reacting to good and bad news** _____
> Why?
> Really?
> That was a good idea!
> Oh, no!
>
> **d Asking about the next part of the story** _____
> What did you do?
> What happened?

4 Pronunciation intonation for responding

▶ 34 Listen to these expressions for reacting to good and bad news. Notice how the speaker uses intonation to show interest. Listen again and repeat.

1 Why?
2 Really?
3 That was a good idea!
4 Oh, no!

5 Work in pairs. Practice the conversation from Exercise 2. Take turns being person A. Pay attention to your intonation when you are responding.

6 Work in pairs. Practice telling a story and responding.

Student A: Use these ideas to tell a story to your partner.

- You had a terrible commute to work.
- You were cycling, and it started raining.
- A car hit your bike.
- You weren't hurt.
- The driver was very nice. He owns a bicycle store.
- He gave you a new bike! It's much better than your old one!

Student B: Listen to your partner and respond with comments and questions.

7 Now change roles.

Student B: Use these ideas to tell a story to your partner.

- You went hiking in the mountains with a friend.
- It started snowing.
- You went back toward the town, but it was getting dark.
- You passed a large house with the lights on.
- The people in the house invited you in. They made you dinner, and you stayed the night.
- The next day, the sun was shining. You reached the top of the mountain.

Student A: Listen to your partner and respond with comments and questions.

8 Think of a bad trip you had. Did it have a happy ending? Make a list of the events. Then tell your partner the story.

4e A story of survival

Writing a short story

1 Work in pairs. What is an interesting story in the news at the moment? Is it good news or bad news?

2 Stories in the news answer some or all of these questions. Read the short story and answer the questions.

1 Where did it happen?
2 What was the weather like? Who was there? What were they doing?
3 What went wrong?
4 What surprising event happened? Who was there? What were they doing?
5 Did the story have a happy or sad ending?

Boys survive 50 DAYS lost at sea

The islands of Atafu are in the middle of the Pacific Ocean, and the people there go fishing every day. One day, the sun was shining and the ocean was calm, so three teenage boys went fishing in a small boat. In the evening, they didn't arrive home, so the islanders went out and looked for them. After many days, there was no sign of them and everyone thought the boys were dead.

Fifty days later, some fishermen were sailing in the middle of the Pacific Ocean when they saw a small boat in the distance. The three boys were in the boat, over 1,500 kilometers (900 miles) from their home. They were living on fish from the ocean and rainwater. In the end, they returned to their families alive and well.

The islands of Atafu

3 Writing skill structure your writing

The story has a five-part structure. Number the parts below in the correct order (1–5).

____ The day the story starts, the background events (such as the weather), and what happened first.

____ An important moment when something goes wrong, and what happens next.

____ There is a happy (or sad) ending.

_1_ The place and the typical lives of the people.

____ A surprising (and often positive) change in the story after a long time.

4 Time expressions help the structure of a story. Look at this example and underline the other time expressions in the story.

> The islands of Atafu are in the middle of the Pacific Ocean, and the people there go fishing <u>every day</u>. <u>One day</u>, the sun was shining and the ocean was calm, so three teenage boys went fishing in a small boat.

5 You are going to write a short story. Use a story from your own life or a story in the news. Plan the story using the five-part structure. Make notes to answer the questions in Exercise 2.

6 Write your short story in about 80–100 words. Use some time expressions to help the structure.

7 Work in pairs. Take turns reading your stories. Does your partner use the five-part structure and time expressions?

4f A microadventure

Alastair and Temujin during their microadventure in Croatia

Before you watch

1 Make a list of things you did in the last 24 hours. Write as many things as you can in two minutes. Then work in pairs. Take turns reading your lists. Who wrote the longer list?

I got up, I brushed my teeth, I ate breakfast, …

2 You are going to watch a video about two friends. They are spending 24 hours in Croatia on a "microadventure." Complete these sentences from the video with the simple past form of the verbs in parentheses.

_____ We _____ (take) a photo of the city lights below.

_____ We _____ (leave) the city.

_____ We _____ (wake up) next to this rock.

_____ We _____ (buy) some bread, some grapes, some meat.

_____ We _____ (go) swimming in the Mediterranean Sea.

_1_ We ___ate___ (eat) ice cream.

_5_ Al _____ (sit) on a wall.

_____ We _____ (have) some water and watched the sunset.

_7_ We _____ (make) a sandwich.

_____ We _____ (find) a river.

While you watch

3 🎦 **4.1** Watch the video. Number the sentences in Exercise 2 in the order they happened (1–10).

4 🎦 **4.1** Watch the video again. Check (✔) the correct options to complete the sentences.

1 Alastair Humphreys is ____ .
- ☐ a filmmaker
- ☐ an adventurer
- ☐ a writer

2 They rented ____ .
- ☐ a car
- ☐ motorcycles
- ☐ bicycles

3 They drove ____ .
- ☐ through a tunnel
- ☐ over a bridge
- ☐ around a bend

4 At the river, they saw ____ .
- ☐ a fish
- ☐ a dragonfly
- ☐ a frog

5 On the top of the mountain, they could hear ____ .
- ☐ people
- ☐ animals
- ☐ music

6 In the morning, Alastair ____ .
- ☐ ate a banana
- ☐ brushed his teeth
- ☐ called his mother

7 Afterwards, they ____ .
- ☐ took a shower
- ☐ had coffee
- ☐ ate breakfast

After you watch

5 Vocabulary in context

🎦 **4.2** Watch the clips from the video. Choose the correct meaning of the words and phrases.

6 🎦 **4.1** Work in pairs. Watch the video again with the sound OFF. Using the simple past tense, describe what happened in the microadventure as you see each action on the screen.

7 Work in pairs. You are going to plan a 24-hour microadventure. Discuss these ideas and make your plans.

- Where will you go?
- What will you do?
- What will you see?

At 9 o'clock, we'll take the train to … and visit …

8 Work with another pair and describe your plans for your microadventure.

A dragonfly

UNIT 4 REVIEW AND MEMORY BOOSTER

Grammar

1 Complete the text with the simple past form of the verbs in parentheses.

In 2013, Aleksander Doba [1]_____ (cross) the Atlantic Ocean in a kayak. He [2]_____ (start) his trip in Lisbon, Portugal, and he [3]_____ (arrive) in Florida six months later. He [4]_____ (travel) 12,427 kilometers (7,722 miles). It [5]_____ (be) a difficult journey. His kayak [6]_____ (break) near the Bahamas, so he [7]_____ (stop) to fix it. He also [8]_____ (have) other challenges—his satellite phone [9]_____ (not work) for 47 days, so he [10]_____ (not have) any communication. Aleksander [11]_____ (be born) in Poland in 1946, and he [12]_____ (not begin) kayaking until the age of 34.

2 **>> MB** Work in pairs. Answer the questions about the story in Exercise 1.

1 What are the personal qualities of Aleksander Doba?
2 Why do you think people like Aleksander take risks and challenge themselves?

3 Circle the correct options.

The sun [1] *shone / was shining* as the plane turned onto the runway. During take-off, the passengers inside the plane sat quietly. They [2] *took / were taking* their first parachute jump. Everyone [3] *was / was being* nervous, and no one [4] *said / was saying* a word. When the plane [5] *reached / was reaching* the correct height, their teacher shouted, "OK, everyone. It's time to jump!" She [6] *opened / was opening* the door on the side of the plane and, in the next moment, everyone [7] *jumped / was jumping* out of the plane toward the ground.

I CAN	
use the simple past and past continuous	☐

Vocabulary

4 Complete the sentences with these words.

challenging	experienced	intelligent
kind	patient	positive

1 Don't get angry when things don't happen as fast as you want. Learn to be _____ .
2 He's a very _____ climber. He started mountaineering when he was a child.
3 It's very _____ of you to help me with my homework.
4 Even when things go wrong, it's important to stay _____ .
5 My friend is the most _____ person in our class. She always gets 100% on tests.
6 Finishing the marathon was very _____ , but I did it in the end.

I CAN	
talk about personal qualities and challenges	☐

Real life

5 **>> MB** Work in pairs. Look at the pictures (1–5).

Student A: Tell the story to your partner using some of these words.

at the beginning	but	luckily	next	while

Student B: Listen to the story and react to good and bad news with some of these phrases.

Oh, no!	Really?	What happened?	Why?

I CAN	
tell a story	☐
react to good and bad news	☐

Unit 5 The environment

Uruguayan artist Jaime built this home in Florianapolis, Brazil, from recycled materials.

FEATURES

58 Recycling

The real story behind recycling our trash

60 Managing the environment

Some environmental stories from around the world

62 A boat made of bottles

How one environmentalist is trying to raise awareness

66 Recycling Cairo

A video about how recycled objects are used in Cairo, Egypt

1 Work in pairs. Look at the photo and the caption. What do you think of the home in the photo? Would you like to stay there? Which of these materials did Jaime use?

| cardboard | glass | leather | metal | paper | plastic | wood |

2 ▶ 35 Work in pairs. Listen to part of a documentary about Jaime and the house in the photo. Answer the questions.

1 What materials does the speaker mention?
2 What did Jaime do with them? Give an example.
3 What does Jaime want people to think about?

3 Work in pairs. Look at the highlighted expressions for talking about objects. Form similar sentences about the everyday objects in the box below.

A dictionary **is made of** *paper.* **You use it for** *looking up words.*

| an envelope | a cell phone | a wallet | a tin can |

4 Think of another everyday object. Don't tell your partner what it is, but describe what it's made of and what you use it for. Your partner has to guess the object.

5a Recycling

Vocabulary recycling

1 Work in pairs. What kind of trash do you throw away or recycle every week? What percentage of each type (a–e) is in your trash can?

About 25% of my trash is paper.

a electronics
b glass
c paper and cardboard
d metal
e plastic

2 Match these objects (1–8) to the type of trash (a–e) in Exercise 1. Some items match two categories.

1 computer _a_
2 bottle _b, e_
3 jar ___
4 aluminum foil ___
5 TV ___
6 cereal box ___
7 magazine ___
8 bag ___

Reading

3 Work in pairs. Look at the photos with the article. What do you think *e-waste* is? Why is the boy holding part of an old computer?

4 Read the article and check your ideas from Exercise 3.

5 Work in pairs. Read the article again and answer these questions.

1 What did Peter Essick find in the markets of Ghana?
2 Why do people melt parts of the broken computers?
3 Why is recycling the metal dangerous?
4 What types of electronic products are environmentally friendly?

▶ 36

Electronic waste in Agbogbloshie dump, Accra, Ghana

E-WASTE

Do you ever throw away any electronic waste (or *e-waste*)? Perhaps you have some old technology that doesn't work, like an out-of-date phone or a slow computer. But when you throw away these objects, do you know where they go? The reporter Peter Essick has followed this e-waste to different countries around the world.

Essick found a lot of e-waste in Ghana, with thousands of old computers in the local markets. Here, the sellers resell a few computers, but they can't sell many because a lot of them don't work. Instead, the sellers melt[1] some parts of the computers to recycle the metal. These parts don't have much metal, but sometimes there is a little gold inside.

Unfortunately, recycling the metal can be dangerous because it produces a lot of chemicals that are bad for workers' health. As a result, Essick thinks we shouldn't send any e-waste to other countries. It's bad for the environment, and it's bad for people's health. He believes we need to produce more environmentally-friendly electronics in the future; in other words, electronic products that you can recycle safely and in the country where they were made or sold.

[1] **melt** (v) /melt/ to heat an object until it turns to liquid

Grammar quantifiers

6 Which of these nouns are countable (C)? Which are uncountable (U)? Write C or U.

trash _U_   computer _C_   plastic ____   bag ____
box ____   magazine ____   paper ____   metal ____

> ▶ **QUANTIFIERS**
>
> We use *quantifiers* with countable and uncountable nouns to talk about quantity.
> *Do you ever throw away **any** electronic waste?*
> *Perhaps you have **some** old technology that doesn't work.*
> *Essick found **a lot of** e-waste in Ghana.*
> *The sellers resell **a few** computers.*
> *They can't sell **many** computers in the market.*
> *These parts don't have **much** metal.*
> *There is **a little** gold inside.*
> *We shouldn't send **any** e-waste to other countries.*
>
> For more information and practice, see page 164.

7 Look at the sentences in the grammar box. Then complete these sentences with the correct quantifiers in **bold** in the grammar box.

1 We use ___*some*___ and ___*a lot of*___ in affirmative statements with countable or uncountable nouns.
2 We use _____ in questions and in negative statements with countable or uncountable nouns.
3 We use _____ to talk about small quantities in affirmative statements with countable nouns.
4 We use _____ to talk about small quantities in affirmative statements with uncountable nouns.
5 We use _____ in negative statements and in questions with countable nouns.
6 We use _____ in negative statements and in questions with uncountable nouns.

8 Circle the correct quantifiers to complete the sentences.

1 How *much / many* trash do you recycle?
2 I recycle *a few / a little* things, like glass and plastic bottles.
3 I don't recycle *many / much* glass.
4 I recycle *a few / a little* paper each week.
5 Do you have *much / any* recycling bins?
6 There are *some / any* old TVs for sale.
7 You shouldn't throw away *many / any* paper!
8 How *many / much* times can paper be recycled?
9 Nowadays, *a lot of / a little* cities and towns have special recycling centers.

Speaking myLife

9 Work in pairs. Discuss these sentences (1–4) about recycling. Are they true for you? If necessary, change the words in **bold** so the sentences are true for you.

1 I throw away **a lot of** paper every week.
2 In my area, **a few** places have recycling bins.
3 My school / place of work **doesn't have any** recycling bins for paper.
4 **Some** people in my country think recycling is important.

*A: How **much** paper do you throw away every week?*
*B: I don't throw away **any** paper. We recycle it in special green bins.*

5b Managing the environment

Vocabulary results and figures

1 Work in pairs. Discuss the questions.

1 How often do you read news about the environment? Is it usually good news or bad news?
2 Do you have any good news about the environment in your country?

2 Read a newspaper report about Portugal. Is it good news or bad news?

> Portugal powered the whole country using only solar, wind, and hydroelectric energy for **about a hundred** hours last week. **Exactly a year** ago, the country produced **under a quarter** of its electricity from wind power, and **nearly half** of its total energy came from renewable energy. So it's a huge achievement for the country to live off renewable energy for **over four days**.

3 Look at the phrases in **bold** in the newspaper report above. Match these phrases with the exact information in a–e below.

a 48% _____
b 107 _____
c from May 7 to May 11 _____
d 22% _____
e 12 months _____

4 Work in pairs. Answer these questions about your life using *over*, *under*, *almost*, and *about*.

1 How much of your day do you spend looking at a screen (e.g., computer, TV)?
   I spend about a third of my day looking at a screen.
2 How many hours a week do you spend shopping?
3 How many people live in your town or city?
4 How much money do you spend on buying clothes each month?
5 How many months a year do you spend at school or at work?

Listening

5 ▶ 37 Work in pairs. Listen to a news report about two environmental projects and answer the questions.

1 What four deserts does the report mention?
2 Where are the two environmental projects?
3 What type of wall are the countries building?

6 ▶ 37 Work in pairs. Listen again and answer the questions.

1 What percentage of the Earth's land is desert?
2 When did the Three-North Shelter Forest Program begin?
3 What is its purpose?
4 How long will the wall be when it's finished in 2050?
5 How many countries are working together on the project in Africa?
6 What are the goals of this project?

Grammar articles

7 Look at the grammar box. Complete these rules (a–c) with *a/an*, *the*, or no article (*x*).

a We normally use _____ when we talk about something that isn't specific or when it's the first time we mention something. When we talk about something specific or talk about it again, we use _____ .

b We also use _____ when something is unique (there is only one), with superlatives, or with the names of some places (e.g., oceans, deserts, mountain ranges).

c We use _____ when we talk about people or things in general, and with the names of most places (e.g., continents, countries, cities, lakes).

8 Read about another way to manage the environment. Circle the correct options. Circle "–" if no article is needed.

Ice towers

In the spring and summer, there is often a water shortage in ¹ *the* / – Himalayan mountains. So during the winter, ² *a* / – people make ice towers. They put one end of ³ *a* / – long pipe into a river high in the mountains, and then they take the other end of ⁴ *a* / *the* pipe down to a village. The water comes out of the pipe and freezes in a fountain to create ⁵ – / *an* ice tower in the village. When the ice tower melts in the spring, ⁶ *a* / – farmers can use it to water their fields.

9 Pronunciation /ðə/ or /ðiː/

a ▶ 38 Listen to the difference in the pronunciation of *the* before a consonant sound and before a vowel sound.

/ðə/	/ðiː/
the wall	the Earth

b ▶ 39 Listen and circle /ðə/ or /ðiː/. Then listen again and repeat.

1 the river   /ðə/   /ðiː/
2 the ice   /ðə/   /ðiː/
3 the world   /ðə/   /ðiː/
4 the desert   /ðə/   /ðiː/
5 the oldest   /ðə/   /ðiː/
6 the largest   /ðə/   /ðiː/
7 the Atacama Desert /ðə/   /ðiː/

10 Work in pairs. Look at these questions from a general knowledge quiz. Complete the questions with *a/an* or *the* where necessary. Then try to answer the questions.

Around the world quiz
1 There is _____ river that flows through parts of _____ Brazil, Colombia, Peru, and Ecuador. What is its name?
2 _____ White House is in _____ USA. Who lives there?
3 There is _____ natural satellite that goes around _____ Earth every day. What is it?
4 In 1998, Larry Page and Sergey Brin set up _____ global search engine. What is its name?
5 _____ Arctic Ocean is _____ smallest ocean in the world. Which is _____ largest?

11 Check the quiz answers on page 155.

Writing and speaking **my Life**

12 You are going to write five more quiz questions. Work in two pairs in a group of four.

Pair A: Turn to page 153 and follow the instructions.

Pair B: Turn to page 154 and follow the instructions.

13 Work in your group. Take turns asking and answering your five questions. Find out which pair has greater general knowledge.

5c A boat made of bottles

Reading

1 Work in pairs. These words and phrases are from the article on page 63. What do you think the article is about?

plastic bottles	special boat	sail
the Pacific Ocean	San Francisco	Sydney

2 Read the article and complete the fact file with numbers about the *Plastiki*.

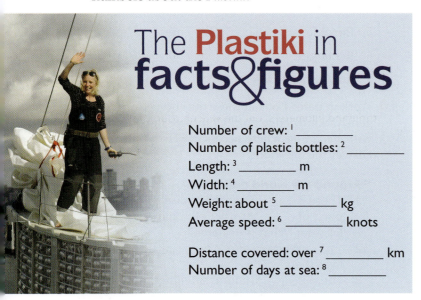

The Plastiki in facts&figures

Number of crew: [1] _____
Number of plastic bottles: [2] _____
Length: [3] _____ m
Width: [4] _____ m
Weight: about [5] _____ kg
Average speed: [6] _____ knots

Distance covered: over [7] _____ km
Number of days at sea: [8] _____

Critical thinking reading closely

3 Read the sentences (1–6). Circle the correct option for each sentence.

T = The sentence is **true**. The information is in the text.
F = The sentence is **false**. The information is in the text.
NG = We don't know if it's true or false. The information is **not given** in the text.

1	The *Plastiki* is made of the same material as other boats.	T	F	NG
2	Humans recycle most of their plastic bottles.	T	F	NG
3	Plastic in the ocean is killing animals.	T	F	NG
4	The *Plastiki* is environmentally friendly.	T	F	NG
5	The size of the "Great Garbage Patch" is growing.	T	F	NG
6	The journey took longer than de Rothschild had planned.	T	F	NG

Word focus *take*

4 Work in pairs. Find and underline five expressions in the article with the word *take*. Then match the expressions with the uses (1–4).

1 transportation: *take a taxi,* _____
_____

2 daily routines: *take a walk,* _____
_____

3 lengths of time: *take a few days,* _____
_____

4 idioms: *take time,* _____
_____

5 Complete the sentences with the correct form of *take* and the words in the box.

a break	many days	care	a plane

1 The work was tiring, and the crew sometimes needed to _____*take a break*_____ and relax.
2 The journey across the Great Garbage Patch was longer than expected—it _____ .
3 Most people _____ from San Francisco to Sydney, so they don't know about the pollution in the ocean.
4 _____ of the environment is a global responsibility.

Speaking *my* **Life**

6 Work in groups and discuss these questions.

1 Do you think environmental projects like the *Plastiki* can make people change their behavior? Why or why not?
2 In your country, does anyone try to change people's behavior in these areas? How do they do this?

- recycling more trash
- stopping smoking
- driving over the speed limit
- eating too much food
- anything else?

The government tries to stop people from smoking cigarettes by ...

A BOAT *made of* BOTTLES

▶ 40

A boat with a difference

1 The *Plastiki* looks similar to many other boats in Sydney Harbour. It's eighteen meters long, six meters wide, and it weighs about twelve thousand kilograms. It carries a crew
5 of six people and has an average speed of five knots.[1] However, once you get near the *Plastiki*, you realize there's a big difference: It's made of twelve thousand five hundred reused plastic bottles.

How did the *Plastiki* begin?

2 10 David de Rothschild is an environmentalist who has crossed Antarctica and explored the Ecuadorian Amazon. One day, he was reading some information about all the plastic in the seas and oceans. He couldn't believe what he was reading. For example, humans throw away four
15 out of every five plastic bottles they use, and plastic trash causes about eighty percent of the pollution in the ocean. In addition, scientists think that around one million seabirds die every
20 year from plastic pollution. De Rothschild decided he wanted to get involved in the fight against ocean pollution. To help more people
25 understand the problem, he started building a boat made of plastic bottles.

Designing the *Plastiki*

3 In addition to building the boat with recycled plastic, it was
30 important to make the boat environmentally friendly and user-friendly. The boat uses renewable energy, such as wind power and solar energy. The crew can make meals with vegetables from the small garden at the back of the boat. They can take a break from work and get some exercise by
35 using the special exercise bicycle. The energy from the bike provides power for the boat's computers. And if anyone needs to take a shower, the boat's shower uses saltwater from the ocean.

The journey

4 40 De Rothschild sailed the *Plastiki* across the Pacific Ocean from San Francisco to Sydney. That's more than fifteen thousand kilometers. On the way, he took the special boat through the "Great Garbage Patch." This is a huge area in the Pacific with 3.5 billion kilograms of trash. You can see
45 every kind of human trash here, but the worst problem is the plastic. It kills birds and ocean life.

How well did the *Plastiki* survive the journey?

5 The journey wasn't always easy, and de Rothschild and his
50 crew had to take care during storms. There were giant ocean waves, and winds of over one hundred kilometers per hour. The whole journey took one hundred and twenty-nine days. Originally, de Rothschild thought the boat could only travel once, but it lasted so well that he is planning to sail it
55 again one day.

[1]**knot** (n) /nɒt/ a measurement of speed at sea (1 knot = 1.8 km/hr)

5d Online shopping

Reading

1 Work in pairs. Do you normally go to stores or do you prefer shopping online? Why?

2 Look at the website and email order. What did the customer order? What is the problem?

WWW.TECOART.COM

| HOME | MY ACCOUNT | SHOPPING CART | CHECKOUT |

We have lots of different clocks, and they are all made from recycled computers!

Computer Hard-Drive Clock with Circuit Board.
$39.00

Apple iPod® Hard-Drive Clock on a Circuit Board.
$35.00

Order number: 80531A

Order date: March 20

Thank you for your order. Unfortunately, the model you ordered is currently not available. We expect more stock to arrive in seven days. We apologize for the delay. For more information about this order, speak to a customer service representative at 555-1754.

Item Number	Description	Quantity	Price
HCV1N	Hard-drive clock	1	$39

Real life calling about an order

3 ▶ **41** The customer is calling customer service about her order. Listen to the conversation. Work in pairs and answer the questions.

1 What information does the customer service representative first ask for and check?
2 Why does the customer want the clock quickly?
3 What does she decide to do?
4 What will the customer service representative email her?

4 ▶ **41** Look at the expressions for calling about an order. Then listen to the conversation again. Circle the sentences the customer service representative uses.

▶ CALLING ABOUT AN ORDER

Telephone expressions
Good morning. How can I help you?
I'm calling about an order for a clock.
Can I put you on hold for a minute?
Is there anything else I can help you with?

Talking about an order
Do you have the order number?
Would you like to order a different product?
Would you like to cancel the order?
Would you like a refund?
Would you like confirmation by email?

Checking and clarifying
Is that A as in America?
Let me check.
So that's F for Freddie?
That's right.

5 Pronunciation sounding friendly

a ▶ **42** Listen to these sentences from a telephone conversation. Does the speaker sound friendly (F) or unfriendly (U)? Circle your answers.

1	Good morning. How can I help you?	F	U
2	Can I put you on hold?	F	U
3	Is that A as in America?	F	U
4	I'm calling about an order.	F	U
5	Is there anything else I can help you with?	F	U
6	Do you have the order number?	F	U

b ▶ **43** Listen to the sentences again. This time, they are all friendly. Work in pairs. Listen and repeat with a similar friendly intonation.

6 Work in pairs. Practice two phone conversations similar to the one in Exercise 3.

Student A: Turn to page 153 and follow the instructions.

Student B: Turn to page 154 and follow the instructions.

A: Good morning. How can I help you?
B: Hello. I'm calling about some clothes I ordered online. I received an email saying ...

5e Emails about an order

Writing emails

1 Read the correspondence between a customer and a customer service representative. Put the emails (A–E) in order (1–5).

A

Dear Mr. Martinez:

I would like to inform you that the e-book reader you ordered is now in stock. I would be delighted to deliver this item immediately. Please reply to confirm you would still like to purchase this item.

Charlotte Lazarro

B

Dear Sir or Madam:

I recently ordered an e-book reader online. However, I received an email that said this was not currently available. Please refund my money back to my credit card.

Yours sincerely,

Carlos Martinez

C

Thanks, but I bought the same product at a store yesterday. Therefore, please cancel the order and, as requested, send me my refund.

Carlos

D

As requested, here is the order number: 80531A

E

Dear Mr. Martinez:

Thank you for your email. I apologize for the difficulties with your order. In order to provide you with the necessary assistance, could you please send me the order number?

Best regards,

Charlotte Lazarro

Customer Service Representative

2 Read the emails in Exercise 1 again. Underline any phrases and expressions that ask for something or give instructions.

3 Writing skill formal words

a The language in the emails in Exercise 1 is quite formal. Match the formal language in the emails to these less formal words (1–9).

1 got   _received_
2 happy   _____
3 asked for   _____
4 give   _____
5 give back (money)   _____
6 help   _____
7 say sorry   _____
8 tell   _____
9 want   _____

b Work in pairs. Make these sentences more formal.

1 I want my money back.
2 I'm writing to tell you that I didn't get the delivery.
3 Do you want any help?
4 Please give us your credit card details.
5 Sorry, but I can't give you your money back.

4 Imagine you ordered a printer online two weeks ago. You paid for delivery within 24 hours, but it hasn't arrived. Write an email to the supplier and request a refund.

5 Work in pairs. Read your partner's email. How formal is the language?

5f Recycling Cairo

Using Egypt's greatest natural resource on the rooftops of Cairo

Before you watch

1 Key vocabulary

Match these words and phrases with the pictures (1–6).

water tank ____	solar panel ____	goat ____
satellite dish ____	rooftop ____	garbage ____

2 Work in pairs. You are going to watch a video about using recycled objects in Cairo. What do you think is the connection between the words and phrases in Exercise 1?

While you watch

3 ▶ 5.1 Watch the video. Were your predictions in Exercise 2 correct?

4 ▶ 5.1 Watch the video again. Work in pairs and answer the questions.

1 How does the narrator describe the streets of Cairo?
2 How does he describe the rooftops of Cairo?
3 What is Thomas Culhane helping Egyptians to do?
4 What is Egypt's great natural resource?
5 What is the new solar hot water system made of?
6 The new solar heaters provide hot water, so what do they reduce?

After you watch

5 Vocabulary in context

▶ 5.2 Watch the clips from the video. Choose the correct meaning of the words and phrases.

6 Write a short summary of the video (about 100 words). Use these phrases.

> People in Cairo use the rooftops for …
> Thomas Culhane is helping some local people to …
> They make the solar water heaters out of …
> The new heaters provide …
> Culhane thinks the solar heaters demonstrate that …

7 ▶ 5.3 Work in pairs. You are going to be the narrator of the video. Watch a shorter version of the video with no sound. Your teacher will play this video twice. As it plays, take turns reading your summary from Exercise 6 to your partner.

8 In the video, Thomas Culhane says, "One man's garbage is another's goldmine." What does he mean by this? Circle a, b, or c.

a Everyone thinks the garbage is worth a lot of money.
b Some people think the garbage is useless, but other people think it's very useful.
c You can sell the garbage for a lot of money.

9 Work in pairs. List some things people often use and throw away that other people could recycle or reuse.

UNIT 5 REVIEW AND MEMORY BOOSTER

Grammar

1 Circle the correct options to complete the article about recycling.

Recycling around the World

A new report looks at recycling in different countries and what they can learn from each other.

Japan

¹ *A / The* Japanese have different types of recycling bins, so local people only throw away ² *a little / a few* household items. For example, they recycle about 100% of their drink cans, which is a lot higher than some countries in ³ *– / the* Europe.

USA

Overall, ⁴ *– / the* USA doesn't recycle as ⁵ *many / much* trash as Japan, but it has introduced ⁶ *a lot of / any* new projects in recent years. This year, it recycled 48% of its paper, 40% of its plastic bottles, and 65% of its cans.

Senegal

Senegal recycles ⁷ *a few / a little* of its waste industrially, but people generally don't throw away ⁸ *any / much* items that they can use for something else. For example, you can buy shoes made from old plastic bags, and drinking cups made from cans.

2 ▶▶ **MB** Work in pairs. Look at the photos. Answer these questions for each photo.

1. What project does the photo show?
2. What is the purpose of this project?

I CAN	
use quantifiers and articles	☐

Vocabulary

3 Work in pairs. What materials are these objects made of?

book	bookshelf	bottle	can
jar	magazine	cell phone	radio

4 ▶▶ **MB** Work in pairs. Think of two more objects for each material in Exercise 3.

5 Look at the percentages in the article in Exercise 1. Match the percentages to these phrases (1–4).

1. a full amount _____
2. just over a third _____
3. about two-thirds _____
4. almost half _____

6 ▶▶ **MB** Write the percentage of time you spend doing these things each day. Then work in pairs. Explain how you spend your time to your partner.

- at work or at school _____
- sleeping _____
- texting friends _____
- watching TV _____
- eating _____

I spend over a third of my day at school.

I CAN	
talk about materials	☐
talk about results and figures	☐

Real life

7 Work in pairs. Practice making a telephone call about an order. Take the roles of someone who works for the company (A) and a customer (B). Use these ideas.

A: Hello. How can / help /?
B: calling / an order / a clock. It hasn't arrived.
A: Do you / order number?
B: It / AG-100234L.
A: Sorry, can / repeat /?
B: Yes, it's /.
A: Let / check. Is / A / America?
B: That's correct.
A: Sorry, this product / currently not in stock. Would / change / order?
B: No. I'd like / refund.
A: That's fine. Would / like confirmation / email?
B: Yes, please.
A: Is / anything else / can help you with?
B: No /. Goodbye.

8 Practice the conversation again, but this time Student B closes their book. Then change roles.

I CAN	
call about an order	☐

Women chat on a station platform in Winterthur, Switzerland.

FEATURES

70 Changing your life

How one couple quit their jobs for a life of adventure

72 World party

Join in some of the world's biggest and most colorful parties

74 Coming of age

A look at how different societies celebrate becoming an adult

78 Steel drums

A video about the steel drums of Trinidad and Tobago

1 The photo shows three generations of people. Check (✓) the three options that describe their stages of life.

- ☐ toddler
- ☐ child
- ☐ teenager
- ☐ young adult
- ☐ middle-aged person
- ☐ elderly person

2 ▶ 44 Work in pairs. Listen to someone talking about the photo. Why does the speaker like the photo?

3 Look at these different life events. Work in pairs and answer the questions.

get your driver's license	buy your first house
get married	go to college or university
leave home	raise a family
start your career	retire from work

1 At what age do people in your country usually do these things?
2 Do you think there is a correct time in your life to do each one?

6a Changing your life

Vocabulary describing age

1 In some countries, it is rude to ask the question "How old are you?" Is it rude to ask this question in your country? When is it appropriate to ask this question? Discuss with a partner.

2 We use the phrases in B to talk about general age (e.g., *He's in his mid-twenties*). Work in pairs. Match the ages in A with the phrases in B.

A				
25	14	83	39	53

B		
early teens	mid-twenties	fifties
late thirties	early eighties	

3 Work in pairs. Think of five famous people you both know. How old do you think they are?

Reading

4 Work in pairs. Read the article on page 71 about Rich and Amanda. How old do you think they were when they quit their jobs? Give reasons for your answer.

5 Work in pairs. Read the article again and answer these questions.

1 What did Rich and Amanda realize they wanted to do?
2 Why did they buy an RV?
3 Where did they plan to travel to by ship?
4 What did their friends think they were crazy to do?
5 What did Rich and Amanda start to do after they left home?

Grammar infinitive forms

> ▶ **INFINITIVE FORMS**
>
> 1 We **intend to leave** our jobs.
> 2 Let's **buy an RV to travel** in.
> 3 It's **difficult to understand** your decision.
>
> For more information and practice, see page 166.

6 Look at the grammar box. Match the sentences (1–3) with the different forms (a–c).

a a verb + an infinitive ____
b an adjective + an infinitive ____
c the infinitive explains the purpose of an action ____

7 Read about three people's future plans. Circle the correct options. How old do you think each person is?

"One day I plan [1] *go / to go* to college, but this year I'm working in a supermarket [2] *earn / to earn* some money. Then I'd [3] *like / to like* to travel around the world for six months."

"I'm so happy [4] *retire / to retire*! Some people tell me I should [5] *relax / to relax* at this stage in my life, but I don't want [6] *sit / to sit* at home doing nothing. I hope [7] *do / to do* some volunteer work."

"These days, it's really difficult [8] *buy / to buy* a house. My husband and I can't [9] *afford / to afford* one, so we're living with his parents and saving money [10] *buy / to buy* a place of our own."

CHANGING your life

▶ 45

Rich and Amanda Ligato were professional people with successful careers. Every week, they worked hard. They always intended to do something fun and exciting on the weekends, but in the end, there was never enough time. One day they asked themselves, "Is this all there is?"

They realized that they wanted to stop working and, instead, to go traveling. Or, as Rich said, "to buy our freedom." But first, they needed to save some money. Every month, they lived on Rich's salary and saved Amanda's. Then they bought an RV to travel from the bottom of South America to Brazil, and from there they hoped to get to Africa on a container ship.

Colleagues at work found it difficult to understand Rich and Amanda's decision. Even their closest friends thought they were crazy to go on this kind of journey. But finally, the day came. Rich and Amanda left their home and started to live their dream.

8 Work in pairs. Look at the correct options in Exercise 7. Which options use the infinitive? Match them to the uses (a–c) in Exercise 6.

9 Match the beginnings of the sentences (1–4) with their endings (a–d).

1 One day, I
2 I'd
3 I want to be good at
4 I want to take a year off

a be happy to live in another country. ____
b intend to buy my own house. ____
c playing the piano. ____
d to travel overseas. ____

10 Pronunciation /tə/

▶ 46 Work in pairs. Listen to the sentences from Exercise 9. Is *to* pronounced /tuː/ or /tə/? Listen again and repeat.

11 Write your own sentences using the sentence beginnings (1–4) in Exercise 9. Then work in pairs. Read your sentences aloud and compare your ideas.

One day, I plan to start my own business.

Speaking my Life

12 Work in pairs. You plan to take six months off and take the trip of a lifetime! Discuss the following questions and make notes about your plans.

- Where do you plan to visit?
- Why do you want to visit these places?
- What type of transportation do you intend to use?
- What do you hope to do in each place?
- What do you think will be easy to do on the trip? What do you think will be difficult to do?

13 Present your trip of a lifetime to the rest of the class.

*We **plan to visit** parts of Asia. First of all, **we want to visit** Vietnam **to see** its beautiful natural attractions, such as …*

WORLD PARTY ▶ 47

People in different countries celebrate Mardi Gras with live music, costumes, fireworks, parades, and lots of good food. The most famous celebrations are in New Orleans, Venice, Rio de Janeiro, and Port-of-Spain.

a Venice, Italy
Mardi Gras is called *Carnevale* in this beautiful city. The first celebrations were in the 11th century, and it is still a big celebration today. Visitors to the city can enjoy the costumes, candles, and fireworks from a gondola in Venice's canals.

b New Orleans, USA
Small parties for Mardi Gras began in the 18th century. By the 19th century they were huge events with masks, costumes, and jazz bands. Visitors should also try "king cake" with its gold, purple, and green decorations.

c Rio de Janeiro, Brazil
The world-famous parades started in the mid-19th century, with decorated floats and thousands of people dancing the samba. People eat a famous meat and bean stew called *feijoada*.

d Port-of-Spain, Trinidad and Tobago
The French arrived here in the 18th century and brought Mardi Gras with them. These days, everyone enjoys the parties and concerts with the famous steel drums playing from morning to midnight.

Reading and vocabulary
celebrations

1 Work in pairs. Which events do you celebrate in your family or country? When do you have parties?

2 Work in pairs. Look at the first paragraph of the article. Why is the article called *World Party*?

3 Read the article. Match the sentences (1–5) with the four cities mentioned in the article (a–d).

1 There were no Mardi Gras celebrations here before the mid-19th century. ____
2 It has the oldest celebration. ____
3 One type of food is decorated with different colors. ____
4 One type of musical instrument is especially important. ____
5 People can travel to the party on a type of boat. ____

4 Find words in the article for these pictures.

1 _____ 2 *floats* 3 _____

4 _____ 5 _____ 6 _____

5 Work in groups. Describe your favorite festival or celebration in your country. Answer these questions.

- When and why did it begin?
- Is there any special food?
- Do people wear special costumes or masks?
- Do people walk around the streets or ride on floats?
- Do you have fireworks at night?
- Is music important? What kind of music is there?

Listening

6 ▶ 48 Listen to a news report about one of the celebrations in the article. Which celebration is it about?

7 ▶ 48 Work in pairs. Listen again. Answer these questions with *Yes*, *No*, or *Don't know* (if the news report doesn't say).

1 Are a lot of people going to come to the celebration?
2 Is Lorette going to dance in the parade?
3 Is Lorette wearing her mask when the interview starts?

Grammar future forms

> **FUTURE FORMS**
>
> 1 *Are you **going to be** in the parade this afternoon?*
> 2 *Everyone **is meeting** at the float at six-fifteen.*
> 3 *Reporter: Do you have a mask?*
>   *Lorette: Sure. Here it is. **I'll put** it on.*
>
> For more information and practice, see page 166.

8 Work in pairs. Look at the grammar box. Answer these questions.

a Which sentence is about an arrangement with other people at a fixed time, made before the conversation?

b Which sentence is about a decision made at the time of speaking?
c Which sentence is about a general plan or future intention? (It was decided before the conversation.)

9 Circle the correct options to complete the sentences.

1 One day when I'm older, I'm *visiting / going to visit* Venice.
2 A: Did Jeff email the times of the parade?
   B: I don't know. *I'll check / I'm checking* my inbox right away.
3 A: Have you bought Mark a present for his birthday?
   B: Yes, *I'm going to / I'll* give him a tie.
4 A: Hey, this costume would look great on you.
   B: Really? I don't think so, but *I'm trying / I'll try* it on.
5 A: What time *will we meet / are we meeting* everyone for the parade?
   B: Julie said to be at the main square at two.

10 Pronunciation contractions

▶ 49 Listen to sentences 1–4 in Exercise 9. Notice how the contractions are pronounced. Listen again and repeat.

11 Complete the sentences with a future form of the verbs in parentheses.

1 At the end of this year, I _____ (quit) my job and write a book.
2 What time _____ we _____ (meet) everyone today?
3 A: My car won't start, and I have a meeting at nine!
   B: Don't worry. I _____ (take) you in my car.
4 I think we also need more decorations for the party, so I _____ (buy) those.

Speaking myLife

12 Work in groups. Imagine your town is going to be five hundred years old. Have a town meeting to plan and prepare the celebration. Discuss this list. Decide what you would like to do, and who is in charge of organizing each item.

- type of celebration
- type of food
- type of music
- type of place
- date and time
- anything else

A: *We're going to have a party with fireworks! I'll buy the fireworks. What about the food?*
B: *I'll buy the food!*

6c Coming of age

Reading

1 Work in pairs. Discuss these questions.

  1 At what age can people legally do these things in your country?

drive a car	get married
buy cigarettes	work full-time
vote	open a bank account

  2 At what age do you think people become adults?

  3 Do you have special celebrations in your country for young people as they become adults?

2 Look at the photos and the title of the article on page 75. What do you think the expression "coming of age" means? Discuss with your partner.

3 Read about the three different coming-of-age ceremonies. Are these sentences true (T) or false (F)?

  1 *Quinceañera* is celebrated in many different countries. T F

  2 The writer thinks the Spanish introduced coming-of-age celebrations to South America. T F

  3 The Hamar groom-to-be must pay money to the bride's family. T F

  4 In Hamar culture, a husband is usually younger than his wife. T F

  5 In Japan, you have more legal rights when you turn twenty years old. T F

  6 The attitudes of some young people toward *Seijin-no-Hi* are changing. T F

4 These pairs of words (1–4) are in the article. Match the words with their definitions (a or b).

  1 country _b_   culture _a_
   a the ideas and customs of a group of people
   b an area of land with its own government

  2 celebration ___   ceremony ___
   a an enjoyable event such as a party
   b a traditional and formal event on a special day

  3 bride ___   groom ___
   a a man on his wedding day
   b a woman on her wedding day

  4 legal rights ___   social traditions ___
   a what the law allows you to do
   b activities or behavior based on the past

Critical thinking analyzing the writer's view

5 The three sections in the article look at the topic in different ways. Match the paragraphs (1–3) with these three ways of looking at the topic (a–c). Underline the words or phrases that help you decide.

  a **Historical view:** The writer includes information about the past. ____

  b **Social view:** The writer includes information about society and how it is changing. ____

  c **Economic view:** The writer includes information about costs. ____

6 Work in pairs and compare your answers.

Word focus *get*

7 Work in pairs. Look at the highlighted word *get* in the article. What word could replace *get* in this expression?

8 Read the description of a wedding. Match the uses of *get* (1–6) with their meanings (a–f).

> Once a couple [1] **gets** engaged, people start to [2] **get ready** for the big day! On the morning of the wedding, everyone [3] **gets up** early. Family and friends sometimes have to travel long distances, but it's a great chance for everyone to [4] **get together**. At the wedding, the bride and groom [5] **get** a lot of presents. When they [6] **get back** from their honeymoon, they move into their new home with all their presents.

a becomes ____		d receive	____
b meet ____		e return	____
c prepare ____		f starts the day	____

Speaking *my* Life

9 Work in pairs. Choose one of these events and describe what happens in your family or country on this day. Try to use the word *get* three times in your description.

a birthday	a religious holiday
New Year's Day	your country's national day
Valentine's Day	another special occasion

COMING of AGE

For some people, the age when you become an adult is the age you learn to drive or leave your parents' home. It can also be when you get married, buy a house, or have children. Or perhaps it's when you finish school and get a job. Different cultures have their own ideas and their own celebrations to symbolize coming of age. 5

Quinceañera

1 In Latin American countries, *Quinceañera* is a well-known celebration for girls around their fifteenth birthday. Attended by
10 family and friends, the festivities include music, food, and dance. Many people believe the celebration started when the Spanish first came to parts of the Caribbean, Central America, and South America. Of course, ancient tribes[1] like the Inca, Maya, and the Aztecs probably already had their own coming-of-age ceremonies,
15 but the Spanish changed these to include European features,[2] such as the *Quinceañera* waltz.[3] This waltz between the teenage girl and her father symbolizes[4] her coming of age.

Bull jumping

2 The Hamar tribe in southern Ethiopia is known for its unique custom
20 of "bull jumping"—part of the coming-of-age ceremony for boys in Hamar culture. A row of fifteen bulls are lined up, and the boy has to jump over them. He must run back and forth twice across the backs of the bulls. The bulls are covered in dung to make them slippery. If the boy falls off, he must wait a year to try again. Hamar men have to
25 do this before they can marry. After choosing a wife, the groom-to-be will have to pay the bride's family a "bride price" of about thirty goats and twenty cows. Because of the costs involved, Hamar men are usually in their mid-thirties and the women aged about seventeen when they marry. As a result, the husband often dies many years
30 before his wife, so many Hamar households are headed by women who have survived their husbands.

Seijin-no-Hi

3 The second Monday of January is a public holiday in Japan. It's a day when all twenty-year-olds are supposed to celebrate their
35 coming of age. Called *Seijin-no-Hi*, the young men and women wear formal clothes and attend ceremonies. Twenty is an important age in Japanese society because you get several adult legal rights, such as the right to vote in elections. However, in recent years, the number of young people celebrating *Seijin-no-Hi* has decreased. This is partly
40 due to Japan's low birth rate, but it could also be because modern twenty-year-olds are less interested in these kinds of social traditions.

[1]**tribe** (n) /traɪb/ a group of people who share the same language and culture
[2]**feature** (n) /ˈfiːtʃər/ a quality or an important part of something
[3]**waltz** (n) /wɔːls/ a traditional and formal dance
[4]**symbolize** (v) /ˈsɪmbəlaɪz/ represent

6d An invitation

Speaking

1 Work in pairs. Which of these events are very formal? Which are less formal? Which could be either?

> a graduation party
> a barbecue with family and friends
> a retirement party for a work colleague
> your grandfather's ninetieth birthday party
> a dinner with a work client

Real life inviting, accepting, and declining

2 ▶ **51** Listen to two conversations. Work in pairs and answer the questions.

Conversation 1
1 What event does Ian invite Abdullah to?
2 Why does Abdullah decline the invitation at first?
3 How does Ian convince Abdullah to come?
4 Does Abdullah need to bring anything?

Conversation 2
5 When is Sally leaving?
6 Where does Joanna invite Sally to?
7 Does Sally accept the invitation?
8 Do you think this conversation is more or less formal than conversation 1? Why?

3 ▶ **51** Look at the expressions below. Listen to the conversations again. Circle the expressions the speakers use.

INVITING, ACCEPTING, and DECLINING	
Less formal	**More formal**
Inviting	
Do you want to …?	Would you like to
How about -*ing*?	come …?
Why don't you …?	I'd like to invite you to / take you to …
Accepting	
It sounds great/nice.	That would be
OK, thanks.	wonderful.
That would be great.	I'd like that very much.
	I'd love to.
Declining	
Thanks, but …	I'd like/love to, but I'm
Sorry, I can't.	afraid I …
	It's very nice of you to ask, but I …

4 Pronunciation emphasizing words

▶ **52** Listen to these sentences. Circle the word with the main stress in each sentence. Then listen again and repeat.

1 I'd love to.
2 That would be wonderful.
3 It's very nice of you to ask.
4 I'd like to, but I'm afraid I'm busy.

5 Work in pairs. Take turns inviting each other to different formal and informal events from Exercise 1. Think about how formal you need to be. Practice accepting and declining.

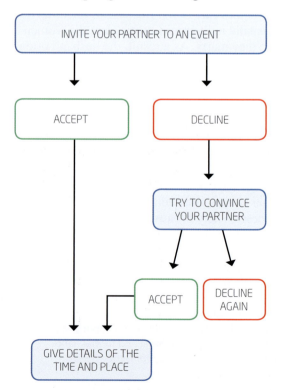

INVITE YOUR PARTNER TO AN EVENT

ACCEPT

DECLINE

TRY TO CONVINCE YOUR PARTNER

ACCEPT

DECLINE AGAIN

GIVE DETAILS OF THE TIME AND PLACE

6e A wedding in Madagascar

Writing a description

1 Read this post from a travel blog. Circle the topics in the box that the writer describes.

food and meals	clothes
people	cities and buildings
music	transportation

Celebrations
IN MADAGASCAR

I was staying in Madagascar with a family, and they invited me to their daughter's wedding. On the big day, I arrived outside an <mark>enormous</mark> tent. There was a zebu (a type of cow) at the entrance brought by the groom. He offered the zebu to the bride's parents to thank them for raising such a <mark>wonderful</mark> daughter. Inside the tent, there were <mark>beautiful</mark> decorations, and over 300 <mark>excited</mark> relatives and guests. The women wore colorful dresses. The older men wore formal suits, but the younger men were less formally dressed. Finally, the ceremony began with some speeches. The crowd listened politely, and sometimes they laughed and clapped. Then the oldest and most respected family members gave the couple their blessing. Finally, it was dinner, and we were served <mark>massive</mark> plates of meat. It was <mark>delicious</mark>! The meal for the bride and groom was served on a special plate, and they ate it using only one spoon to show that they were now joined as one. After the ceremony, the couple went back to their new home to begin their life together.

2 Writing skill descriptive adjectives

a When you write about places or special events, it's important to use interesting and very descriptive adjectives. Match the highlighted adjectives in the travel blog with these less descriptive adjectives (1–3).

1 big __*enormous*__ , _____
2 nice __*wonderful*__ , _____ , _____
3 happy _____

> ▶ **WORDBUILDING synonyms**
>
> Some words have the same meaning, or a similar meaning. These are called synonyms.
> *old = ancient, big = huge, boring = dull*
> Using synonyms can improve a description and make it more interesting to read.
>
> For more practice, see Workbook page 51.

b Work in pairs. Improve these sentences with more descriptive adjectives. You can use the words above or your own ideas.

        beautiful   *ancient*
1 Istanbul is a ~~nice~~ city with lots of ~~old~~ buildings.
2 The USA is a big country. It will take days to drive across it.
3 The parade was kind of boring after a while.
4 The crowd was happy because the fireworks had started.
5 All the costumes were nice.
6 I tried sushi for the first time, and it was really good.

c Work in pairs. Look at the topics in the box in Exercise 1. Think of two or three interesting adjectives for each one. Use a dictionary to help you. Then work with another pair and compare your adjectives.

food and meals: delicious, tasty, disgusting

3 Choose one of the topics below and write a short description (one paragraph) for a travel blog.

- a day you remember from a holiday
- your favorite place in the world
- a hotel you stayed at recently
- a festival or celebration

4 Work in pairs. Read your partner's description. Does it include interesting adjectives?

6f Steel drums

A steel drumming competition in Port-of-Spain during Trinidad and Tobago's Carnival celebrations

Before you watch

1 Work in pairs. Look at the photo on page 78 and discuss these questions.

1 What kind of musical instrument is the woman playing?
2 How important is music in your country?
3 Does your country have a traditional type of music and musical instrument?

2 Key vocabulary

Read the sentences (1–5). The words and phrases in **bold** are used in the video. Write these words and phrases next to their definitions (a–e).

1 Before you can play a guitar, you have to **tune** it.
2 Young children are **influenced** by their parents.
3 Oil companies store and transport the oil in **drums**.
4 In most countries, smoking is **banned** in public places.
5 The didgeridoo is a long wooden musical instrument. It's **native to** the aboriginal people of Australia.

a comes from _____
b affected or changed _____
c round metal containers _____
d not allowed (by law) _____
e change the sound of an instrument so it sounds nice _____

While you watch

3 ▶ **6.1** Watch the video. Number these actions in the order you see them (1–4).

____ Beverly and Dove learn to play the drums.
____ Children and adults play together in a steel band.
____ Tony Poyer says that the steel drum, or pan, was invented in Trinidad and Tobago.
____ Honey Boy tunes a drum.

4 ▶ **6.1** Watch the video again. Work in pairs and answer the questions.

1 What are the islands of the Caribbean region famous for?
2 According to Tony Poyer, when was the steel pan invented?
3 Why did Trinidad have many oil drums?
4 Do most steel drum musicians play by reading music?
5 Who do you find in a "panyard"?

After you watch

5 Vocabulary in context

a ▶ **6.2** Watch the clips from the video. Choose the correct meaning of the words and phrases.

b Complete the information about the Australian didgeridoo with these words and phrases.

| play by ear | performers | backgrounds |
| goes back | escape | |

The didgeridoo is a musical instrument that
¹ _____ about 1,500 years. It is made from a long piece of wood with a hole down the middle. Aborigines of different tribes and ² _____ play the didgeridoo. They don't read from music but ³ _____ . As you travel around Australia, you can't ⁴ _____ its famous sound. You'll often see ⁵ _____ playing the instrument at special Aboriginal celebrations because it's an important symbol of their culture.

6 Work in pairs and discuss these questions.

1 Musical instruments can be important national and cultural symbols. What are some other important symbols of your country or culture?
2 Plan a two-minute video about your country's symbols. Which ones will you show in the video? What will you say about them?
3 Present your idea for the video to the class.

UNIT 6 REVIEW AND MEMORY BOOSTER

Grammar

1 >> **MB** Work in pairs. Look at these sentences about the future. Can you explain the difference in meaning between the different verb forms?

1 I'm going to major in English in college.
2 I think I'll study for my English test next.
3 I'm meeting my friend at two o'clock to study English together.
4 I plan to study English in college.

2 Circle the correct options to complete the sentences.

1 We *hope* / *'re going to* visit my family this weekend.
2 A: I need someone to carry these books for me.
   B: I *'m helping* / *'ll help* you!
3 It isn't easy *win* / *to win* the lottery.
4 A: When *are you going to start* / *starting* your homework?
   B: In a few minutes.
5 Rachel *will have* / *is having* a party tonight. She planned it months ago.

3 >> **MB** Work in pairs. Tell each other about:

- your plans for this weekend.
- your future career intentions.

I CAN	
use infinitive forms	☐
use different future forms	☐

Vocabulary

4 Work in pairs. Match the verbs in A with the words in B to make phrases.

A	go	learn	buy	raise

B	a house	to school	to drive	a family

5 >> **MB** Work in pairs. Look at the phrases in Exercise 4 and answer these questions.

1 In what order do these things typically happen in life?
2 Which things have you done?
3 How old were you when you did them?
4 How did you feel at the time?
5 When do you plan to do the other things?

6 Complete the text about the Asakusa Samba Carnival with these words.

costumes	decorations	drums	floats	parade

Every year on the last Saturday of August, over 500,000 people gather in Tokyo for the Asakusa Samba Carnival. The [1] _____ starts on Umamichi Street and lasts for about five hours. A music group beats out a rhythm on a variety of [2] _____ . Samba teams from all over the country wear bright, glittering [3] _____ . The performers dance in the streets and ride on large [4] _____ that are covered in colorful [5] _____ .

I CAN	
talk about age and the stages of life	☐
talk about parties and celebrations	☐

Real life

7 Look at the sentences (1–3). Replace the phrases in **bold** with these phrases in the box.

I'd like to	that sounds	would you like to

1 **Why don't you** come with me to the movies?
2 **It's nice of you to ask**, but I won't be home this evening.
3 Thanks. **That'd be** great.

8 Work in pairs. Take turns inviting each other to do something this week. Accept or decline the invitation.

I CAN	
invite people and accept or decline invitations	☐

How well do you sleep?

Mostly A answers:
The average human needs around eight hours of sleep per night. You probably get this because you usually sleep very well. You have regular routines, and you are hardly ever tired.

Mostly B answers:
You sleep quite well. Maybe you wake up once or twice a night and that's normal. But you have a busy life, so you need extra hours in bed. Try to go to bed early during the week, and sleep an extra hour over the weekends.

Mostly C answers:
You work hard and get home late, and sometimes work in the evening at home, so you probably don't get the sleep you need. Try to relax in the evening and go to bed early.

UNIT 5b Exercise 12, page 61

Pair A

Write questions for these answers or use your own ideas (e.g., write questions about your own country).

 Buckingham Palace
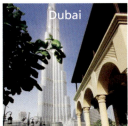 Dubai
 Easter Island
 the Sphinx
 Facebook

UNIT 5d Exercise 6, page 64

Student A

1 You ordered some clothes online. You received an email from the company. The clothes are not in stock. Call the customer service helpline.

- Say why you are calling.
- Your order number is EI3304A.
- Spell your last name.
- Find out how long you have to wait for the clothes.
- Ask for a refund. The price was $149.50.

2 You are a customer service assistant for a book supplier. Answer the telephone.

- Ask for the customer's order number and the title of the book.
- The book isn't in stock. You don't know when the book will arrive.
- Offer the caller a second-hand copy of the same book. It's $3.50.

UNIT 5b Exercise 12, page 61

Pair B

Write questions for these answers or use your own ideas (e.g., write questions about your own country).

the sun

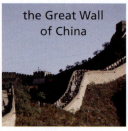
the Great Wall of China

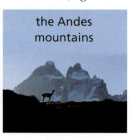
the Andes mountains

Twitter

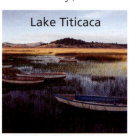
Lake Titicaca

UNIT 5d Exercise 6, page 64

Student B

1 You are a customer service representative for a clothing company supplier. Answer the telephone.

- Ask for the customer's order number and his / her last name.
- The clothes aren't in stock, but they will be in two weeks.
- Offer some different clothes at the same price.

2 You ordered a book online called *Learn Spanish in One Week*. You received an email from the company. The book is not in stock. Call the customer service helpline.

- Say why you are calling.
- Your order number is AZE880.
- Find out how long you have to wait for the book.
- Ask for the price of the second-hand copy.
- Buy the second-hand book.

UNIT 1e Exercise 3b, page 17

1 DOB = Date of birth, No. = number,
   etc. = et cetera (Latin for "and the rest"),
   e.g. = for example
2 *Mr.* is used before the name of any man.
   Mrs. is used before the name of a married woman.
   Ms. is used before the name of a woman when we
   don't know if she is married or single, or if she
   prefers not to say.
   Dr. means Doctor.
3 Form B: It says "Please use capital letters" at
   the top.

UNIT 4c Exercise 1, page 50

The riddle: The answer is "your name."
The matchstick puzzle: Move two matches.

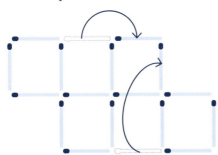

The numbers memory challenge: Most people can
remember up to the seven numbers in 7430673, but
find it difficult to remember eight numbers or more.

UNIT 5b Exercise 11, page 61

1 the Amazon River
2 the president of the United States
3 the moon
4 Google
5 the Pacific Ocean

GRAMMAR SUMMARY UNIT 1

Simple present and adverbs of frequency

Use

We use the simple present:

- to talk about habits and routines.
  *I **play** tennis every week.*

- to talk about things that are always true.
  *Sleep **is** really important for health.*

Form

We form the simple present with the base form of the verb. To make negative sentences, we add *don't* before the verb. To make questions, we add *do* before the subject.

After *he, she, it*, etc., we add *-s* to the verb. We use *doesn't* in negative sentences, and *does* in questions.

	+	–	?
I/you/we/they	I *eat.*	You *don't eat.*	*Do* you *eat?*
he/she/it	She *eats.*	He *doesn't eat.*	*Does* he/she/it *eat?*

The verb *be* is different from other verbs.

	+	–	?
I	*I'm fit.*	*I'm **not** fit.*	*Am* I *fit?*
you/we/they	*We're fit.*	*They **aren't** fit.*	*Are* you *fit?*
he/she/it	*She's fit.*	*She **isn't** fit.*	*Is* he *fit?*

▶ **Exercise 1**

Adverbs and expressions of frequency

We use adverbs and other expressions in simple present sentences to talk about how often we do things.

> *Mike **usually** goes for a run in the evening.*
> *I'm **often** late for work.*
> *I have a hot drink **five or six times a day**.*
> *We go on vacation **two or three times a year**.*

Some common frequency adverbs are:

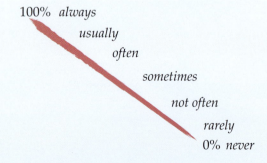

100% *always*
      usually
      often
      sometimes
      not often
      rarely
0%   *never*

Position

Frequency adverbs and expressions of frequency go in different places in a sentence.

- Adverbs of frequency go before the main verb, but after the verb *be*.
  *They **never** <u>eat</u> out.*
  *She'<u>s</u> **always** out on the weekend.*
  *I **don't often** <u>play</u> sports.*

- Expressions of frequency normally go at the beginning or end of a sentence.
  *I go out with friends **three or four times a week**.*
  ***Once a week**, I go for a run.*

▶ **Exercises 2 and 3**

Present continuous

Use

We use the simple present to talk about things we do or that happen regularly. We use the present continuous to talk about something in progress in the present. This can be:

- something actually in progress at this moment.
  *I can't answer the phone because I'm **driving**.*

- something happening around now, but not necessarily at this moment.
  *I'm **looking** for a new job.*

- a changing situation.
  *More and more people **are changing** their diet.*

Form

We form the present continuous with *be* + verb + *-ing*.

	+	–	?
I	*I'm writing.*	*I'm **not** writing.*	*Am* I *writing?*
you/we/they	*We're writing.*	*They **aren't** writing.*	*Are* you *writing?*
he/she/it	*He's writing.*	*She **isn't** writing.*	*Is* she *writing?*

Some verbs describe states (for example, *agree, believe, own, hate, know, like, love, prefer, want*). We don't use these verbs with the continuous.

> ~~*He's owning a really nice car.*~~
> *He **owns** a really nice car.*

▶ **Exercises 4, 5, and 6**

Exercises

1 Complete the sentences with the simple present form of the verbs in parentheses.

1 Sam _____ (not live) near me.
2 Sofia _____ (drive) to work.
3 _____ she _____ (speak) any other languages?
4 I _____ (not like) waking up early.
5 _____ they _____ (see) each other on the weekends?
6 We _____ (be) very tired.
7 Some people _____ (not need) a lot of sleep.
8 _____ (be) your bus late?
9 He _____ (have) a big house in the country.

2 Look at the sentences. Find and correct the mistakes with the position of frequency adverbs and time expressions.

1 I often am tired at work.

2 We twice a week eat out in a restaurant.

3 I have two or three times a day a cup of coffee.

4 They don't play often board games.

5 Does usually she take public transportation?

3 Complete the text with words from the boxes. Use an expression from box A and a verb from box B in each pair of blanks.

A			
~~always~~	every day	often	rarely
two or three times a month			

B			
eat (x2)	~~get up~~	go	meet

I ¹_____*always*_____ ²_____*get up*_____
at about 7:30 a.m. and get ready for work.
I ³_____ ⁴_____
breakfast because I don't feel hungry in the mornings. I start work at 9 a.m., and at 12 noon I take a lunch break. I ⁵_____
⁶_____ my friend for lunch—normally two or three times a week. At 1:30 I start work again, and I finish at 5:30 p.m.
I like to keep fit, so I ⁷_____ to the gym ⁸_____ . I get home at about 8:00 p.m. and make dinner, but
I also ⁹_____ at restaurants
¹⁰_____ . I'm always tired in the evenings, so I go to bed early. And that's my day!

4 Complete the sentences with the present continuous form of these verbs.

become	build	go	not work
talk	wait	write	

1 I _____ for the bus.
2 A: Where _____ you _____ ?
   B: To the supermarket. We need milk!
3 She _____ this week because she's on vacation.
4 A: What are you doing?
   B: I _____ an email to my friend.
5 A: Where's Michael?
   B: He _____ to someone on the phone.
6 They _____ a new house on my street.
7 More and more people _____ vegetarians.

5 Complete the pairs of sentences with the verbs in parentheses. Use the simple present form in one sentence and the present continuous form in the other.

1 I _____ my lunch very early today.
   I normally _____ at 1 p.m. (eat)
2 Tina rarely _____ to work. But today she _____ because of the rain. (drive)
3 She _____ to her brother on the phone right now. They _____ at this time every day. (talk)
4 It's 6 p.m. and I _____ hard in the office. I normally _____ only until 5 p.m. (work)
5 I _____ shopping now. I always _____ shopping at this time. (go)

6 Complete the text with the simple present or present continuous form of the verbs in parentheses.

The Mediterranean diet

People in countries like Italy, Spain, France, and Greece ¹_____ (live) longer than people from many other countries. This is probably because of their diet—they ²_____ (eat) lots of food like vegetables, fruits, nuts, beans, fish, and olive oil. People often ³_____ (say) that this diet ⁴_____ (be) good for your heart. But the traditional Mediterranean diet ⁵_____ (change) because more and more people ⁶_____ (eat) junk food. So, in the future, the Mediterranean diet might be very different.

GRAMMAR SUMMARY UNIT 2

Modal verbs for rules

Use

To talk about rules, we use the modal verbs *must,* *have to,* and *can.*

- To say that something is obligatory, we use *must* or *have to.*
  You **have to** train hard to run a marathon.
  Runners **must** arrive twenty minutes before the race.

- To say that something is allowed, we use *can.*
  Members **can** use the swimming pool for free.

- To say that something is not obligatory but allowed, we use *don't have to.*
  You **don't have to** be fit to join the club.

- To say that something is not allowed, we use *can't* or *must not.*
  You **can't** touch the ball with your hands or arms in soccer.
  You **must not** leave any bags in this area.

The modal verbs *must* and *have to,* and *can't* and *must not,* have very similar meanings. In general, we prefer to use *have to* and *can't* in spoken English to talk about rules. In formal written English, we prefer to use *must* and *must not.*

> You **have to** pay $40 to be in the race. (spoken)
> Competitors **must** pay $40 to enter the race. (formal, written)
> You **can't** go near the pool with shoes on. (spoken)
> Customers **must not** go near the pool with shoes on. (formal, written)

But remember that *must not* and *don't have to* have completely different meanings—*mustn't* means "don't do it!," while *don't have to* means "it's not necessary to do it."

Form

We normally use modal verbs before a main verb.
> You **can** <u>borrow</u> my running shoes.

The modal verbs *must/must not* and *can/can't* don't work like normal verbs. They never change—we use the same form for all persons (*I, you, he/she/it,* etc.). We don't use *do, does,* or *did* to make questions or negatives.

	+	−	?
I/you/we/they	*I* **can** *swim.*	*I* **can't** *swim.*	**Can** *you swim?*
he/she/it	*She* **can** *swim.*	*He* **can't** *swim.*	**Can** *he swim?*

The modal verb *have to* works like a normal verb. It changes for *he/she/it* in the simple present, and we form questions and negatives in the past and present using *do, does,* or *did.*

	+	−	?
I/you/we/they	*I* **have to** *go.*	*I* **don't have to** *go.*	**Do** *you* **have to** *go?*
he/she/it	*He* **has to** *go.*	*She* **doesn't have to** *go.*	**Does** *she* **have to** *go?*

▶ **Exercises 1, 2, and 3**

-ing form

We use the *-ing* form of a verb after *be* to form the present or past continuous.
> I'm **getting** ready to go out.
> I was **watching** a movie.

However, we also use the *-ing* form in some other ways.

-ing form as the subject of a sentence

We can make a verb the subject of a sentence. When we do this, we usually use the *-ing* form.
> **Playing** sports is great for your health.

-ing form after prepositions

When a verb comes after a preposition, it is always in the *-ing* form.
> I'm not very good <u>at</u> **swimming**.

-ing form after some verbs

We sometimes put two verbs together in a sentence. The form of the second verb depends on the first verb. After the verbs *like, dislike, love, hate, can't stand, enjoy,* and *don't mind,* the second verb is in the *-ing* form.
> Jan <u>loves</u> **watching** sports.
> I <u>don't mind</u> **running** in the cold.

▶ **Exercises 4 and 5**

Exercises

1 Match the rules (1–6) with the meanings (a–c).

a Do this.
b Don't do this.
c This is allowed.

1 You must wear your seat belt in a car. ____
2 You can't hit the ball with your hand in soccer. ____
3 Boxers have to wear special gloves. ____
4 You can walk in a marathon. ____
5 The students can't use their cell phones during the exam. ____
6 We can take photos during the tennis match. ____

2 Circle the correct options to complete the sentences.

1 You *must not / don't have to* kick the ball when you play basketball. You can only use your hands.
2 We *must not / don't have to* go to the football game. We can watch it on television.
3 If the fire alarm rings, you *must / don't have to* go straight outside. It's important to be quick.
4 In many countries, you *must / must not* wait until you are 18 to drive. It's not possible if you're younger.
5 You *don't have to / must not* come tonight. Stay at home if you prefer.

3 Circle the correct options to complete this email.

How are you? I'm doing well. You asked me in your email about the gym I go to, so here's some information for you. You ¹ *have to / must* pay for a whole month—you ² *don't have to / can't* pay for one visit. When you pay, they give you a gym card. You ³ *don't have to / must not* forget this card because you need it to get in the gym.

I like to use the bikes in the gym. I usually ride for about an hour, but when there are a lot of people, you ⁴ *can't / must not* use the bikes for a long time. I also do a yoga class once or twice a week. You ⁵ *don't have to / must not* sign up in advance, so I usually decide when I arrive. One last thing—you ⁶ *must / can't* remember to bring towels with you because the gym doesn't give them to you.

Why don't you come with me to the gym next week? I can show you everything. Let me know!

4 Complete the sentences with the *-ing* form of a verb from the box.

fail	play	help	watch	wake up	read

1 She's really good at _____ the piano.
2 I don't like _____ TV—it's so boring!
3 He hates _____ early on the weekends.
4 I'm worried about _____ my exam.
5 _____ a book is a great way to pass the time on a train.
6 Thank you for _____ me with my work.

5 Circle the correct options to complete the conversation.

A: Why are you ¹ *cleaning / clean* the house?
B: It's dirty. Why?
A: It's such a nice day. Why don't we ² *doing / do* something outside? ³ *Staying / Stay* at home is so boring.
B: OK. What do you think about ⁴ *go / going* for a run?
A: I hate ⁵ *run / running*!
B: OK, how about ⁶ *going / go* for a walk in the mountains?
A: That's a good idea. We could ⁷ *taking / take* a picnic with us.
B: Great! I love ⁸ *eat / eating* outside on a sunny day.
A: Good—you can ⁹ *making / make* the picnic for us, then!

GRAMMAR SUMMARY UNIT 3

Comparatives and superlatives

Form

Adjective	Comparative	Superlative
slow	slower	(the) slowest
easy	easier	(the) easiest
difficult	more difficult	(the) most difficult
good	better	(the) best

For most **one-syllable adjectives**, we add *-er* to form the comparative, and we add *-est* to form the superlative.

> *fast → fast**er** / fast**est***   *old → old**er** / old**est***

For most adjectives that have **two or more syllables**, we use ***more*** + adjective to form the comparative, and we use ***most*** + adjective to form the superlative.

> *useful → **more** useful / **most** useful*
> *expensive → **more** expensive / **most** expensive*

For **some two-syllable adjectives** (often adjectives that end in *-y, -le, -ow,* and *-er*), we can use either *-er* or *more* to form the comparative, and *-est* or *most* to form the superlative. We sometimes use one form more than the other (e.g., *narrower* is more common than *more narrow*, whereas *friendlier* and *more friendly* are both common).

> *friendly → friendlier* or *more friendly*
>   *friendliest* or *most friendly*
> *simple → simpler* or *more simple*
>   *simplest* or *most simple*
> *narrow → narrower* or *more narrow*
>   *narrowest* or *most narrow*

Spelling rules

Note the following spelling rules when adding *-er* or *-est* to adjectives.

- For adjectives that end in *-e*, we just add *-r* or *-st*.
  nice → nicer / nicest
- For adjectives that end in *-y*, we change the *y* to *i* and add *-er* or *-est*.
  busy → busier / busiest
- For one-syllable adjectives that end in consonant-vowel-consonant, we generally double the final consonant.
  big → bigger / biggest   *wet → wetter / wettest*
  However, we do <u>not</u> double *w, x,* or *y.*
  slow → slower / slowest

Irregular forms

There are three common irregular adjectives.

> *good → better / best*
> *bad → worse / worst*
> *far → further* or *farther / furthest* or *farthest*

Less and *the least*

To make a negative comparison, we use *less +* adjective to form the comparative, and *the least +* adjective to form the superlative.

> *fun → **less** fun / **the least** fun*
> *popular → **less** popular / **the least** popular*

Use

We use comparative adjectives to compare things. We often use it with *than.*

> *A taxi will be **quicker than** a bus.*
> *We could get a bus, but a taxi will be **quicker.***
> *This one's **more expensive than** the others.*
> *They're **less popular than** they used to be.*

We use superlative adjectives to compare one thing with other things in a group. We usually use *the* before a superlative.

> *What's **the easiest** way to get to the center of town?*

We can also use a possessive form (*the company's, New York's, my,* etc.) and words such as *the second, the third, the next,* etc., before a superlative.

> *Times Square is **New York City's busiest** subway station and Grand Central is **the second busiest**.*

▶ **Exercises 1 and 2**

as ... as

We use *as +* adjective *+ as* to say things are the same.

> *Riding a bike there is **as quick as** going by bus.*
> *It's **as old as** I am.*

To say things are not the same, we use *not as +* adjective *+ as.* The thing we mention first is smaller or less busy / heavy, etc.

> *The UK is **not as big as** Italy.*
> *The town is**n't as busy as** it used to be.*

▶ **Exercises 3 and 4**

Comparative modifiers

We use comparative modifiers when we say there is a big or small difference between things that we are comparing.

To say there is a **big difference**, we can use *a lot* or *much*.
To say there is a **small difference**, we can use *a bit* or *a little*.

> *Public transportation is **much more expensive** than it used to be.*
> *Lucy's house is **a bit closer** than Sue's.*
> *We usually fly from Manchester if possible—Heathrow Airport is **a lot less convenient**.*
> *Our new car is **a little bigger** than our old one.*

▶ **Exercise 5**

Exercises

1 Complete the sentences with the comparative or superlative form of the adjectives in **bold**.

1 I've driven lots of **nice** cars, but this one is the _____ .

2 Chicago is pretty **far** from here, but Boston is _____ .

3 Today's lecture was **interesting**, but I think last week's was _____ .

4 I've flown with some **bad** airlines, but SpeedAir has to be the _____ ever!

5 The exhibition is **busy** today, but yesterday was _____ . In fact, I think yesterday was the _____ day so far since it opened.

6 I'm pretty **good** at tennis, but my friend Alex is _____ . Actually, he's probably the _____ player in the club.

7 Peru is a **big** country, but Argentina is _____ . In fact, Argentina is the second _____ country in South America, after Brazil.

2 Complete the transportation facts. Use the comparative or superlative form of the adjectives in parentheses. Add *the* or *than* if you need to.

1 _____*The fastest*_____ (fast) time taken to visit all the world's countries by public transportation is 4 years and 31 days.

The world's ² _____ (long) and ³ _____ (deep) rail tunnel, the Gotthard Tunnel in Switzerland, opened in 2016. It is 57 km long, and is about 3 km ⁴ _____ (long) the Seikan Tunnel in Japan.

The country with ⁵ _____ (high) number of train passengers is China with over 17 billion rail journeys per year. This is much ⁶ _____ (high) India with 8 billion.

3 Write sentences using *as … as* and an adjective from the box.

big	fast	heavy	~~high~~

1 Height: Mount Fuji 3,776 m, Mount Kilimanjaro 5,895 m
   Mount Fuji isn't as high as Mount Kilimanjaro.

2 Area: USA 9,833,634 km², Canada 9,984,670 km²
   _____

3 Top speed: Kangaroo 71 kmh, Horse 71 kmh
   _____

4 Weight: Jumbo Jet 180,000 kg, Dreamliner 120,000 kg
   _____

4 Rewrite the sentences using *as … as* so that the meaning is the same.

1 Traveling by car is safer than traveling by motorcycle.
   Traveling by motorcycle isn't as safe as traveling by car.

2 Riding a bike and driving are both dangerous. They have the same number of accidents.
   _____
   _____

3 Heathrow Airport is more convenient for us than Gatwick Airport.
   _____
   _____

4 Going by car is no quicker than taking the bus.
   _____
   _____

5 Complete the text about travel in Indonesia. Use the comparative or superlative form of the adjectives in parentheses. Add any other words you need.

¹ _____ (good) way to travel around Indonesia depends on where you are. On major islands, getting around is generally ² _____ (much / easy). Away from the tourist areas, it can be ³ _____ (bit / difficult).

Buses are ⁴ _____ (convenient) and popular means of transportation in Indonesia. Between major tourist destinations, air-conditioned buses are available, and these buses are generally ⁵ _____ (quick). However, prices can be ⁶ _____ (lot / high) the slower local buses.

Trains run only in Java and in parts of Sumatra. They're ⁷ _____ (bit / expensive) the bus, but are ⁸ _____ (much / quick), and it's worth paying extra for a ⁹ _____ (comfortable) journey.

GRAMMAR SUMMARY UNIT 4

Simple past

Use

We use the simple past to talk about finished actions, events, or situations in the past.

> I **visited** the Taj Mahal last year.
> We **saw** a great movie over the weekend.

Form

Simple past forms can be regular or irregular.

- We form the simple past of regular verbs by adding -ed to the base form of the verb.
  *want → want**ed***   *look → look**ed***

- If the verb ends in -e, we just add -d.
  *like → lik**ed***   *hope → hop**ed***

- We form the simple past of verbs ending in consonant + -y by changing -y to -ied.
  *study → stud**ied***   *try → tr**ied***

- We don't form the simple past of irregular verbs with -ed.
  go → went   *hear → heard*   *see → saw*

For a list of common irregular simple past forms, see page 180.

To form negatives in the simple past, we use *didn't* + base form of the verb.

	+	–
I/you/we/they	*I* **watched.**	*I* **didn't watch.**
he/she/it	*He* **watched.**	*She* **didn't watch.**

The verb *be* is different from other verbs. Its simple past form is *was* or *were*. We don't use *didn't* to form negatives.

	+	–
I/he/she/it	*I* **was** *tired.*	*She* **wasn't** *tired.*
you/we/they	*We* **were** *tired.*	*You* **weren't** *tired.*

▶ **Exercises 1 and 2**

Simple past questions

We make questions in the simple past with *did* + base form of the verb.

> Why **did** you **choose** to visit Turkey?
> **Did** she **have** fun on vacation?

When we make questions in the simple past with the verb *be*, we use *was* or *were*. We do not add *did*.

> **Were** you tired after your trip?
> Where **was** your hotel?

▶ **Exercise 3**

Past continuous and simple past

Use

We use the past continuous to talk about an action in progress at a moment in the past.

> I **was watching** TV at eight o'clock last night.
> Tony **was living** in Madrid in 2015.

Form

We form the past continuous with *was/were* and the -ing form of the main verb.

	+	–	?
I/he/she/it	*I* **was** **reading.**	*He* **wasn't** **reading.**	**Was** *she* **reading?**
you/we/they	*They* **were** **reading.**	*We* **weren't** **reading.**	**Were** *you* **reading?**

We often use the past continuous and the simple past together. We use the past continuous for a longer, continuing activity, and the simple past for a shorter, finished action.

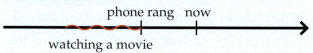

> Jack **was watching** a movie when his phone **rang**.
> I **met** my husband when I **was traveling** around India.

We often use *when* and *while* to join the two parts of a sentence with past continuous and simple past together. We use *when* before a simple past or a past continuous verb. We normally only use *while* with a past continuous verb.

> I met Matthew **when** I was living in California.
> Someone stole my camera **while** I was eating in a restaurant.

When we use *when* with the simple past, it can also mean "after."

> I called Sylvia **when** I read her message.

If the part of the sentence with *when* or *while* comes first, we put a comma after it.

> **When** I met Matthew, I was living in California.

Remember that we don't use verbs that describe states (e.g., *believe, like, love, prefer, know*) with a continuous tense.

▶ **Exercises 4, 5, and 6**

Exercises

1 Complete the second sentence in each pair with the simple past form of the verb in **bold**.

1 She **wants** to travel the world.
   She _____ to travel the world.
2 It **isn't** easy to get a job.
   It _____ easy to get a job.
3 They **don't have** a lot of money.
   They _____ a lot of money.
4 He **doesn't like** traveling by plane.
   He _____ traveling by plane.
5 They **are** late again.
   They _____ late again.
6 I **study** in the school library.
   I _____ in the school library.

2 Complete the text with the simple past form of these verbs. One verb is used twice.

hire	be	visit	decide
drive	not know	eat	not want

An island vacation … with a difference

Last summer, my husband and I ¹_____ the island of Sicily in Italy. We love the water, but we ²_____ to spend every day on the beach. So, we ³_____ to go to Mount Etna, a live volcano! We ⁴_____ to the mountain from our hotel early in the morning. When we arrived, we ⁵_____ where to go, so we ⁶_____ a guide to help us. She ⁷_____ very good and told us about the history of the volcano. When we got near the crater, there was a strong smell, but the views at the top ⁸_____ amazing. After that, we went back to the hotel and ⁹_____ a delicious lunch there. It was a fantastic experience!

3 Write simple past questions with these words.

1 how / be / your hotel?
   _____
2 when / you / get back?
   _____
3 they / take the train home?
   _____
4 what / be / your / favorite experience?
   _____
5 you / call me / this morning?
   _____
6 how much / your / plane tickets cost?
   _____

4 Complete the sentences with the past continuous form of the verbs in parentheses.

1 We _____ (wait) for the bus.
2 He _____ (not eat) his food.
3 _____ you _____ (talk) to your friend?
4 What _____ those people _____ (say) to each other?
5 It _____ (not rain) when we left the house.
6 Where _____ she _____ (fly) to?

5 Circle the correct options to complete the sentences.

1 Jack *arrived / was arriving* while I *was watching / watched* TV.
2 When the taxi *arrived / was arriving*, we *got / were getting* in.
3 It *was starting / started* snowing while we *climbed / were climbing* the mountain.
4 He *wasn't playing / didn't play* on his computer when I *was seeing / saw* him.
5 *Did she ski / Was she skiing* when she *had / was having* the accident?
6 I *knew / was knowing* he had a problem when I *heard / was hearing* him shout.

6 Complete the text with the simple past or past continuous form of these verbs.

not end	come	eat	look
reach	start	travel	wait

I had an amazing surprise while I ¹_____ around India last year. I ²_____ dinner in a restaurant in Delhi when someone ³_____ in and sat at the table next to me. She ⁴_____ familiar, but I couldn't remember who she was. We ⁵_____ talking, and then I realized—it was Maggie, my best friend from elementary school!

But the story ⁶_____ there. When I ⁷_____ the airport on the last day of my vacation, who did I see there? Maggie, of course. She ⁸_____ for the same flight, and her seat was right in front of mine on the plane!

GRAMMAR SUMMARY UNIT 5

Quantifiers

We use quantifiers with nouns to talk about quantity. The choice of quantifier depends on:

- if the noun is countable or uncountable.

- if we are talking about small or large quantities.

Some nouns are countable. This means they can become plural, for example, *computer, bag, box, magazine*. Other nouns are uncountable. This means they cannot normally become plural, for example, *trash, plastic, paper, metal*.

Quantity	Countable	Uncountable
large quantity	*a lot of / lots of*	*a lot of / lots of*
neutral quantity (not large or small)	*some*	*some*
small quantity	*not many*	*not much*
small quantity	*a few*	*a little*
no quantity (zero)	*not any*	*not any*

We use *a lot of* or *lots of* with countable and uncountable nouns to talk about large quantities.
> There was **a lot of** trash on the streets after the party.
> We have **lots of** great shops in my neighborhood.

We use *some* with both countable and uncountable nouns. It does not refer to a specific amount—we use it to talk about quantities that are not large and are not small.
> I found **some** really useful books in the library.
> (= not a lot)

In more formal English, we use *many* + plural noun to talk about large quantities.
> There are **many** interesting places to visit in the city.

We also use *many* and *much* in questions.
> Are there **many** good shops where you live?
> Do you have **much** free time?

We don't normally use *many* and *much* in affirmative sentences in spoken English. We use *a lot of* or *lots of* instead.

We use *not much* and *not many* to talk about small quantities. We use *not much* with uncountable nouns and *not many* with plural countable nouns.
> There weren't **many** people at the party.
> They don't have **much** money.

Note that *not* always goes with the verb in the sentence.

We also use *a few* and *a little* to talk about small quantities. We use *a few* with plural countable nouns and *a little* with uncountable nouns.
> I have **a few** really good friends.
> There's **a little** milk in the container.

We use *not any* with countable and uncountable nouns to talk about zero quantity (when there is nothing).
> I don't have **any** money.
> There weren't **any** shops open when we arrived.

Note that *not* always goes with the verb in the sentence.

We also use *any* with countable and uncountable nouns to ask questions.
> Are there **any** good beaches in the area?
> Do you have **any** orange juice?

▶ **Exercises 1, 2, and 3**

Articles (*a/an*, *the*, or no article)

We use *a/an*:

- to talk about something that isn't specific.
  *Have you got **a** pen?* (not a particular pen)

- the first time we mention something.
  *I saw **an** eagle yesterday.*

We use *the*:

- the second time we mention something.
  A man and a woman were waiting for us at the airport.
  ***The** man helped us with our suitcases.*

- when something is unique.
  ***The** sun looked really beautiful from the top of the mountain.*

- with superlatives.
  *It was **the best** vacation of my life.*

- with the names of some places, such as oceans (e.g., ***the** Atlantic Ocean*), deserts (e.g., ***the** Sahara Desert*), and mountain ranges (e.g., ***the** Himalayas*).

We use no article:

- to talk about plural or uncountable nouns in general.
  I never stay in (–) hotels because they're so expensive.
  (–) Tourism brings a lot of money to the area.

- with the names of most places, for example, the names of continents, countries, cities, and lakes.

▶ **Exercises 4, 5, and 6**

Exercises

1 Choose one quantifier from each pair to complete the sentences.

1 many / much
   a There wasn't _____ cheese in the fridge.
   b There weren't _____ apples left.
2 a little / a few
   a There was _____ space for me on the seat.
   b We have _____ recycling bins outside our house.
3 many / much
   a How _____ tea do you drink in a day?
   b How _____ tourists visit the national park?
4 some / any
   a The parking lot didn't have _____ space for my car.
   b _____ people prefer shopping online.

2 Circle the correct option (a–c).

1 I can't travel this year because I don't have _____ money.
   a much   b a lot   c few
2 The hotel doesn't have _____ free rooms.
   a some   b any   c a little
3 I have _____ clothes I don't wear.
   a a lot   b lots of   c much
4 He made _____ coffee for me.
   a any   b many   c some
5 There was _____ trash left in the trashcan.
   a a few   b a little   c little
6 The shop had _____ things that I liked.
   a much   b a little   c a few

3 Circle the correct options to complete the conversation.

A: Wait! Don't throw your coffee cup in the trash.
B: Why not?
A: Well, if [1] *a lot of / a little* people throw away their coffee cups, it creates [2] *a few / lots of* trash.
B: I only drink [3] *a little / a few* cups of coffee a week. That's not [4] *much / many* coffee cups.
A: Yes, but I read in an article that people throw away 7 million coffee cups every day in the US!
B: Really? That is [5] *a lot of / a little* cups!
A: I know. The article says that [6] *some / any* businesses now have recycling bins for coffee cups.
B: Were there [7] *much / any* recycling bins in the café we were in?
A: Look, here's one! You can recycle your cup here.

4 Circle *a, an, the,* or no article (–) to complete these facts.

Surprising facts about our world
1 Redwood trees are *the / –* tallest trees in the world.
2 *– / The* Lake Superior is the largest lake in the USA.
3 China built *the / an* amazing bridge over the Dehang Canyon. *The / A* bridge is the highest in the world.
4 Mercury is the closest planet to *– / the* sun.
5 *– / The* honey bees only live for five to six weeks.
6 Until around 4,000 years ago, *the / –* Sahara Desert was green, and animals probably lived there.

5 Circle *a, an, the,* or no article (–) to complete the conversation.

A: I watched [1] *an / the* interesting documentary last night about [2] *the / –* flowers.
B: Really?
A: Yeah. [3] *The / A* documentary showed where in [4] *– / the* world they grow [5] *the / a* flowers and how they arrive here in the US.
B: And what did you learn?
A: Well, they grow the flowers in countries like [6] *– / the* Kenya, and then they ship them around the world.
B: That's not great for [7] *a / the* environment. Did you learn anything else?
A: Yeah. Most of our flowers come from [8] *the / a* big market in the Netherlands. It's [9] *a / the* biggest flower market in the world!

6 Circle *the, a,* or no article (–) in the text below.

In [1] *a / the* small town called Rjukan in [2] *the / –* Norway, there is no sunlight for six months a year. People in [3] *the / –* Rjukan live without [4] *the / a* sun from September to March. But this is changing, thanks to Martin Andersen—a local man who had the clever idea to use [5] *a / the* mirror to bring sunlight to the town. [6] *The / A* mirror is on top of a mountain next to the town, and it reflects light from the sun onto [7] *a / the* town's main square. [8] *The / –* people love coming to the main square and sitting in the sun.

GRAMMAR SUMMARY UNIT 6

Infinitive forms

An infinitive is defined as *to* + base form of the verb. We use infinitive forms in different situations.

verb + infinitive

Sometimes, two verbs appear together in a sentence. The form of the second verb depends on the first verb. Many verbs (e.g., *decide, help, hope, intend, learn, need, plan, pretend, promise, want, would like*) are followed by infinitives.

> I *need to go* to the store.
> We *decided to move* abroad.

adjective + infinitive

When a verb appears after an adjective, it is often in the infinitive form.

> It's *exciting to visit* new places.
> It's *nice to see* you again.

▶ **Exercise 1**

infinitive explaining the purpose of an action

We also use the infinitive form to say why we do something.

> I went to the library *to look* for a book.
> She's going to Paris *to visit* a friend.

We don't use *for* + verb to give reasons.

> ~~I called Jan *for invite* her to my party.~~
> I called Jan *to invite* her to my party.

Note that the negative form of an infinitive is *not to* + base form of the verb.

> I promise *not to do* that again.
> It's important *not to work* too hard.

See Unit 2 for when we use the *-ing* form of a verb.

▶ **Exercises 2 and 3**

Future forms

Present continuous

We use the present continuous to talk about a fixed arrangement in the future, for example, when we have planned something with other people or when we have already spent money. We normally mention a specific time.

> We're *getting* the train at 11:20 a.m.
> I'm *going* to the theater with Michelle tonight.

be going to

We use *be going to* + base form of the verb to talk about general plans and intentions.

> I'm *going to travel* around Asia this summer.
> We're *going to go* to the movies this weekend.

We form questions and negatives with *going to* in the same way as in the present continuous.

> I'm *not going to have* time to see you.
> Are you *going to drive* to the party?

will

We use *will* + base form of the verb when we make a decision while we're speaking.

> A: *What can I bring you?*
> B: *I'll have* the tuna salad, please.

We also use *will* to make promises and offers.

> We'll *meet* you at the train station.
> I'll *pay* for your ticket.

▶ **Exercises 4, 5, and 6**

Exercises

1 Complete the text with the infinitive form of the verbs in the box.

go	complete	pursue	stay

Yesterday was a special day for Michael Sanders. At the age of 75, he finished his college degree. "I always intended [1] _____ to college," says Michael. "But when I finished high school, I decided [2] _____ my career, not study." However, Michael always had his dream, and he didn't give up. He was 70 years old when he started college, and it wasn't easy. "I often found it hard [3] _____ my work on time," he says. "But the other students were great. They helped me a lot." And Michael's not finished—he hopes [4] _____ in college for a few more years and get another degree.

2 Match the beginnings of the sentences (1–5) with the endings (a–e).

1 I'm saving money
2 She went to the university library
3 Let's go to the gym
4 I looked out of the window
5 You need to study hard

a to buy a new car. ____
b to exercise. ____
c to pass your exam. ____
d to see the weather. ____
e to study. ____

3 Circle the correct options to complete the sentences.

1 I can't stand *staying / to stay* inside all day.
2 I think it's easy *learning / to learn* a new language.
3 Jack helped me *to fix / fixing* my car.
4 I would like *to visit / visiting* China one day.
5 I'm not very good at *to paint / painting*.
6 I went to the store *for buying / to buy* some milk.
7 *Eating / To eat* vegetables is good for your health.
8 I was happy *hearing / to hear* about your new job.

4 Complete the sentences with the *be going to* form of these verbs.

come	not get	have	miss
~~watch~~	spend	start	

1 I *'m going to watch* that new crime drama tonight.
2 _____ you _____ to our party tomorrow?
3 Tanja _____ a baby in December.
4 Mathieu _____ six months in Australia later this year.
5 I _____ married until I'm at least 30!
6 _____ we _____ our train?
7 I _____ college in September.

5 Circle the correct options to complete the dialogs.

1 A: This bag's heavy.
   B: *I'll help / I'm helping* you to carry it!
2 A: Do you have plans for tonight?
   B: *I'm going / I'll go* to the movies. I just bought my ticket.
3 A: There's no more milk!
   B: Oh, no! *I'm going / I'll go* to the store and get some.
4 A: I can't wait until the exams are over.
   B: I know. *I'm going to take / I'll take* a vacation after my exams.

6 Choose the best explanation (a or b) for each sentence (1–4).

1 I'm meeting my friend John at 4:30 p.m.
   a We planned this together.
   b This is an idea, but I'm not totally sure.
2 I'm going to travel when I finish college.
   a I've already decided where to go, and I've booked some hotels.
   b This is my idea, but I haven't booked anything yet.
3 It's raining. I'll take you to the store in my car.
   a I just decided this now.
   b We organized this earlier.
4 I'm going to join a gym this month.
   a I made an appointment at a gym for this Friday at 10 a.m.
   b This is my idea, but I haven't organized anything yet.

Irregular verb chart

VERB	SIMPLE PAST	PAST PARTICIPLE
be	was / were	been
become	became	become
begin	began	begun
bring	brought	brought
build	built	built
buy	bought	bought
choose	chose	chosen
come	came	come
cost	cost	cost
do	did	done
drink	drank	drunk
eat	ate	eaten
fall	fell	fallen
feel	felt	felt
find	found	found
fly	flew	flown
forget	forgot	forgotten
get	got	gotten
give	gave	given
go	went	gone
grow	grew	grown
have	had	had
hear	heard	heard
hurt	hurt	hurt
keep	kept	kept
know	knew	known

VERB	SIMPLE PAST	PAST PARTICIPLE
leave	left	left
let	let	let
lose	lost	lost
make	made	made
meet	met	met
pay	paid	paid
put	put	put
read	read	read
run	ran	run
say	said	said
see	saw	seen
sell	sold	sold
send	sent	sent
sit	sat	sat
sleep	slept	slept
speak	spoke	spoken
spend	spent	spent
swim	swam	swum
take	took	taken
teach	taught	taught
tell	told	told
think	thought	thought
understand	understood	understood
wake	woke	woken
wear	wore	worn
write	wrote	written

Unit 1

▶ 1

Normally, national parks are in the countryside. But Bukhansan National Park in South Korea is part of the city of Seoul. It's about forty-five minutes from the city center by subway. About ten million people visit the park every year. People in Seoul go walking there on the weekends. It's a good way to relax.

▶ 5

P = Presenter, D = David McLain
(The words of David McLain are spoken by an actor.)

P: No one knows exactly the reason why some people live longer than others. Why are they so healthy? Is it their diet? Do they go to the gym more than other people? Well, one man is trying to answer these questions— photographer David McLain. He's currently traveling to different places around the world that have large numbers of people over a hundred years old and asking the question: Why are they so healthy? At the moment, he's working on the island of Sardinia in Italy, and he's speaking to us right now on the phone. David, thank you for joining us today.
D: Hello.
P: So, first of all, tell us why you decided to visit Sardinia.
D: Well, Sardinia is an interesting place because men live to the same age as women. That isn't normal for most countries. Men normally die younger.
P: And does anyone know the reason why men live longer in Sardinia?
D: There are different ideas about this. One explanation is that family is so important here. Every Sunday, the whole family eats a big meal together. Research shows that in countries where people live longer, family is important.
P: I see. So, do you think people live longer in traditional societies?
D: That's an interesting question. Sardinia is a very traditional place, but, even here, the younger generation are eating more food like French fries and burgers. Also, young people are moving to the city, so they are exercising less because of their lifestyle. It'll be interesting to see what happens in Sardinia in the next twenty or thirty years.

▶ 8

C = Customer, P = Pharmacist
1
P: Hello, how can I help you?
C: Hello. I have a runny nose and a sore throat. I feel terrible.
P: Do you have a temperature as well?
C: No, it's normal.
P: Well, you should take this medicine three times a day. It's good for a sore throat.
C: Thanks.
P: And try drinking hot water with honey and lemon. That helps.
C: OK, I will.
P: Oh, and why don't you buy some cough drops? They should help. If you still feel sick in a few days, see a doctor.

P = Patient, D = Doctor
2
D: Good morning. What seems to be the problem?
P: I have a backache.
D: OK, how did you hurt it?
P: I was lifting something heavy, and my back suddenly started hurting.
D: I see. Do you feel any pain when I press on it like this?
P: Not too much, but I can't stand or walk for too long.
D: OK, I'll give you something for the pain. Take one tablet twice a day for seven days. Stay in bed and get some rest. If the pain doesn't go away by next week, come back and see me again.

Unit 2

▶ 9

An Ironman competition has three different races. In the swimming race, the competitors swim for 3.86 kilometers. Then they cycle for 180 kilometers, and finally they run a marathon. The world final of the Ironman Championship is held annually in Hawaii, and it's very competitive. Every year, around 1,900 people compete against each other in front of thousands of spectators.

▶ 11

1
Learning to win and lose is important in a child's education because it teaches them about life. So I think competitive sports in schools are good for children. They're also good for physical health, because when children try to win, they work harder and get more exercise. The other good thing about competitive sports is that children learn to work well in teams when they play against another team. Competitions are a great lesson in teamwork.
2
Some children aren't good at sports, so when school sports are competitive, they always lose. That's really bad for the child. The fact is that not all children are the same, and some children don't like sports. I think schools in my country should be more like the schools in Finland. They are successful schools, but they aren't competitive. They don't have competitive sports, either. So when a child can't do a sport very well, that's OK as long as they do their best and try hard at everything they do.
3
We have a sports day at my school and the children love it. Yes, winning is nice for a child, but the whole day is also a lot of fun. So, overall, I don't think there's a problem with having competitive sports in schools—the problem is with some of the parents. Some parents hate losing and get very competitive. When there's a race or a game, some of them shout at their kids. They think it's the Olympic Games or something!

▶ **12**

A: What's on TV?
B: Cycling. It's the Tour de France. I love watching it.
A: Oh, no! I think it's boring!
B: I disagree. I really enjoy watching the cyclists ride through the mountains.
A: Sitting in front of the TV all day isn't exciting. I'm tired of doing nothing. Are you any good at tennis? We could play this afternoon.
B: But I want to watch this.
A: What's wrong? Are you afraid of losing?

▶ **13**

1 thing
2 win
3 bank
4 sing
5 ran
6 pink

▶ **15**

A: Hey! Have you seen this?
B: What?
A: This ad. You're really good at taking photos.
B: I have so much work at the moment. I don't have time for this.
A: But you could win a new camera!
B: I can take nice photos of friends and family, but I'm not really very creative about it.
A: OK. Well, how about joining something else? Er, this one! Are you interested in acting?
B: You're kidding. I hate standing up in front of people. You're more of a performer than I am.
A: Yes, but it's a musical. I'm not very good at singing.
B: Let me see that. But it says here enthusiasm is more important than talent. You should do it. I think you'd enjoy it.
A: Mm, well, maybe. But I think I'd prefer to join this one on Wednesday evenings.
B: What? You? Exercise?
A: What do you mean? Anyway, it looks like fun. Why don't you come too?
B: But I'm so out of shape!
A: That's the whole point. There's a beginner's group. You should do it with me.

Unit 3

▶ **17**

This photo was taken on a train in Bangladesh. It was the end of Ramadan, and lots of people travel home at that time of year. Train tickets sell out quickly, so you often see people riding on top of the trains and between the carriages. In this picture, the woman is sitting between the carriages because there isn't space on top of the train. It looks dangerous, but she doesn't look very worried.

▶ **19**

A: Sorry I'm late. Eight-thirty in the morning is the worst time for traffic.
B: I know what you mean. My bicycle is faster than your car during rush hour!
A: I'm sure it is, but I travel farther than you. It'd take me hours to get here by bicycle.
B: There's also the cost of gas. It's so expensive!
A: Tell me about it! In fact, last week I went to look at an electric car.
B: Good idea. They're better for the environment.
A: They're better, but they're also more expensive.
B: Really? Well, what about public transportation? Isn't there a bus stop near your house?
A: Yes, but the fastest bus takes over an hour. It has so many stops!

▶ **21**

When we talk about transportation, most people think of buses, cars, bicycles, and so on. But in some parts of the world, animal transportation is as popular as these modern vehicles, and sometimes more popular. In fact, at certain times of the year, animals are the only way to travel. Take the desert, for example, with its 50 degrees Celsius temperatures. Yes, you can cross it in the right vehicles, but for long distances, modern vehicles are not as good as camels. A camel can travel over 40 kilometers per day and can go without water for three to five days. Yes, it's slower, and maybe a camel isn't as comfortable as a car. But a camel's big feet make it more reliable in the sand—unlike a car, it doesn't get stuck.

In winter, northern Alaska can be as cold as the North Pole. Temperatures go down to minus 50 degrees Celsius. Engines can freeze, and even if your car starts, snow and ice on the road can make driving impossible. When the weather is as bad as this, the only way to travel is by sled with a team of between six and eight huskies. These famous dogs can pull heavy sleds for hundreds of kilometers. There is even a race for huskies in Alaska called the Iditarod, where large teams of huskies pull sleds over 1,600 kilometers.

▶ **24**

J = Javier, D = Driver
1
J: Hello. Are you free?
D: Yes, where are you going?
J: I'd like to go to the station, please.
D: Bus or train?
J: Oh, sorry. The train station.
D: OK. Hop in.

2
D: There is road construction up by the entrance.
J: You can stop here. It's fine. How much is that?
D: Six thirty.
J: Sorry, I only have a twenty-dollar bill. Do you have change?
D: Sure. So, that's thirteen seventy. Do you want a receipt?
J: No, it's OK, thanks. Bye.

S = Shelley, D = Driver

3

S: Hi. Do you stop at the airport?

D: Yes, I do. Which terminal are you going to? North or south?

S: Um. I need to get to the … north terminal.

D: OK. A one-way or round-trip ticket?

S: One way, please.

D: That's two dollars.

J = Javier, T = Ticket office clerk

4

J: A round-trip ticket to the airport, please.

T: OK. The next train leaves in five minutes.

J: Right. That one, please.

T: First or second class?

J: Second.

T: OK. That's fourteen dollars fifty cents.

J: Oh, no! I don't think I have enough cash.

T: Credit card is fine.

J: Great. Here's my card.

T: OK. Here you are.

J: Which platform is it?

T: Um, platform six.

A = Attendant, S = Shelley, J = Javier

5

A: Hello. Can I see your passport?

S: Here you are.

A: Thanks. How many bags are you checking in?

S: None. I only have this carry-on.

A: OK. Window or aisle seat?

S: Err, I don't really care, but can I get a seat next to my friend?

A: Has he already checked in?

S: No, I'm waiting for him.

A: Well, I can't …

J: Shelley!

S: Javier! Where have you been?

J: It's a long story.

Unit 4

▶ **26**

My name's Vic, and I live in Tennessee. During the week, I work in a bank. I like my job, but most of the time I'm sitting at a desk, so I need to get some exercise after work and on the weekends. Most people go running or play sports, but I like caving. My co-workers think I'm a little crazy because they say it's dangerous. It's true that sometimes you have to take a risk when you go caving, but I always go with other cavers, and we look out for each other. It's important to work as a team when you go down into a new cave, because every cave gives you a different challenge. The most difficult cave I've explored is Rumbling Falls Cave. You have to use a rope to climb down a hole that's about twenty meters into the ground. At the bottom, you are on your hands and knees for nearly a kilometer, so you need to be physically fit. Then, at the end, you come into the main part of the cave. It's an incredible place, like a huge room. Getting to Rumbling Falls Cave is probably my biggest achievement as a caver so far.

▶ **29**

In May 1985, Joe Simpson and Simon Yates climbed the Siula Grande mountain in the Andes. It's a dangerous mountain, but Simpson and Yates were very experienced climbers and felt optimistic about the challenge. The sun was shining when they left their tents on the first day, and everything went well. Three days later, they reached the top of the mountain, but they didn't stay there long. It was snowing, and the weather was getting worse. While they were going down the mountain, Simpson fell and broke his knee. Yates tied a rope between them and slowly lowered Simpson down the mountain with the rope. Sometime later, when they were getting closer to the bottom of the mountain, Simpson slipped and fell over a cliff. For an hour, Yates held the rope while his friend was hanging in the air. But the rope was getting too heavy, and it was pulling Yates off the mountain. Simon Yates had an impossible decision: Either he could hold the rope, but then they might both die, or he could cut the rope and save himself. …

▶ **30**

(The first part of the story is repeated from track 29.)

… At the last second, Yates cut the rope. The next day, he looked for his friend, but couldn't find him. Sadly, Yates decided he was dead. But amazingly, Simpson was still alive, and he started to crawl towards their camp. Three days later, Yates was sleeping in his tent. He planned to go home the next morning. But at midnight, he suddenly woke up. Someone was shouting his name. He ran outside and looked everywhere. Finally, he found Simpson on the ground. He wasn't moving, but he was still breathing. Yates carried him to the tent, and Simpson survived. Later, their story became famous as a book and a movie.

▶ **31**

1   I was working on my own when a group of people came into my office.

2   We met them when they were living above our apartment.

3   They weren't getting along very well, so the team agreed to have a meeting.

4   The weather was cold this morning, but it wasn't raining.

▶ **33**

A: Hi, Mark. How was your camping trip?

B: It was great in the end, but we had a terrible time at the beginning.

A: Why?

B: First, we left the house late, and then after only half an hour, the car broke down.

A: Oh, no! What did you do?

B: Fortunately, there was a garage nearby and the mechanic fixed the problem. But when we arrived at the forest, it was getting dark. After we drove around for about an hour, we finally found the campsite, but it was completely dark by then. And it was raining!

A: Really? So what happened?

B: We found a nice, warm hotel down the road!

A: That was lucky!

B: Yes, it was a great hotel. In the end, we stayed there for the whole weekend.

A: Sounds great!

Unit 5

▶ 35

Every day we throw away objects such as wood, old household appliances, and glass bottles. But an artist from Uruguay called Jaime built a house made from these types of objects. The house is in Brazil, and it has a bedroom, a kitchen, and a bathroom. There are shelves made from trees and old wood, and there's lots of light. That's because Jaime used colored glass from bottles in the walls. When people visit the house, Jaime wants them to think about the environment and about how we recycle and reuse everyday objects.

▶ 37

Nearly thirty percent of the land on Earth is desert. While the ice in the two cold deserts of the Arctic and Antarctica is starting to melt, hot deserts such as the Gobi Desert and the Sahara are getting bigger. Some countries are trying to stop these deserts from expanding.

Take China, for example. People know about the Great Wall of China, but China is planning on building another wall—this time of trees. Known as the Three-North Shelter Forest Program, the project began in 1978. China started planting the wall of trees to stop the Gobi Desert from spreading toward the cities of northern China. Now the wall has about 66 billion trees, and by 2050 it will be 4,500 kilometers long with about 100 billion trees.

There is a similar problem with the Sahara Desert, which is the largest hot desert in the world. Twenty-one countries in Africa are working together to build a "Great Green Wall" against the spread of the Sahara. The wall of trees is meant to improve food security, create jobs, and restore 50 million hectares of land.

▶ 41

V = Recorded voice, C = Customer service representative, J = Jane

V: Thank you for calling Teco Art dot com. Your call is important to us. For information about our latest products, press one. For orders, press two. For problems with your order, press three. … All our customer service representatives are busy. We apologize for the delay. Your call is important to us. One of our customer service representatives will be with you as soon as possible.

C: Good morning. How can I help you?

J: Hi, I'm calling about an order for a Computer Circuit Board Clock from your website. I received an email saying I have to wait seven more days.

C: One moment … Do you have the order number?

J: Yes, it's 8-0-5-3-1-A.

C: Is that A as in America?

J: That's right.

C: Is that Ms. Jane Tan of 90 North Lane?

J: Yes, it is.

C: Hmm. Can I put you on hold for a minute?

J: Sure.

C: Hello?

J: Yes, hello.

C: I'm very sorry, but this product isn't in stock at the moment. We'll have it in seven days.

J: I already know that. But it's my husband's birthday tomorrow.

C: Ah, I see. Well, would you like to order a similar clock? We have an Apple iPod one for thirty-five dollars.

J: Hmm. I really like the one I ordered.

C: Oh, I'm sorry about that. Would you like to cancel the order?

J: Yes, I think so. How does that work?

C: We'll refund the amount of thirty-nine dollars to your credit card.

J: OK. Thanks.

C: And would you like confirmation by email?

J: Yes, please.

C: Let me check. Your email is J Tan at gmail dot com.

J: That's right.

C: Is there anything else I can help you with?

J: No, thanks. That's everything.

C: OK. Goodbye.

J: Bye.

Unit 6

▶ 44

These three people are waiting in a train station in Winterthur, Switzerland. I like the picture because it shows three people at different stages of their lives communicating in different ways. The elderly woman and the middle-aged woman are chatting, and the young woman—she looks like she's in her twenties—is probably texting her friends or using social media.

▶ 46

1 One day, I intend to buy my own house.
2 I'd be happy to live in another country.
3 I want to be good at playing the piano.
4 I want to take a year off to travel overseas.

▶ 48

R = Reporter, L = Lorette

R: It's about six o'clock in the morning here in New Orleans, and the streets are very quiet. But in about six hours, the city is going to have the biggest party in the world, with thousands of visitors from all over. However, Mardi Gras is really about the local communities in the city. So, I've come to the traditional Tremé neighborhood of New Orleans, where there are already some people preparing for the big day. So, I'll try to speak to some of them … Hello? Hello?

L: Hello?

R: Hello. What's your name?

L: Lorette.

R: Hi, Lorette. You're wearing a fantastic costume. Are you going to be in the parade this afternoon?

L: Yes. Everyone is meeting at the float at six-fifteen, and then we're going to ride through the city.

R: As I say, your dress looks amazing. Did you make it?

L: Yes, we all make our own costumes for Mardi Gras.

R: And do you have a mask?

L: Sure. Here it is. I'll put it on.

R: Wow! That's perfect. So tell me—how important is Mardi Gras for the people in Tremé?

L: It's the most important event of the year. It brings people together.

R: Well, good luck this afternoon. You're going to have a great time, I'm sure!

1 One day when I'm older, I'm going to visit Venice.
2 A: Did Jeff email the times of the parade?
   B: I don't know. I'll check my inbox right away.
3 A: Have you bought Mark a present for his birthday?
   B: Yes, I'm going to give him a tie.
4 A: Hey, this costume would look great on you.
   B: Really? I don't think so, but I'll try it on.

I = Ian, A = Abdullah
1

I: Hi, Abdullah. How's it going?
A: Good, thanks, Ian. I've finished all my classes today, so I can relax. I think I'll take it easy this weekend.
I: Why don't you come to my house on Saturday? My family's having a barbecue in the back yard. It'll be fun.
A: Thanks, but I have a few things to do at home. Besides, it's with your family, so you probably don't want other people there …
I: No, really. I'm inviting a few other people from school as well, so you'll know some people there. I'd really like you to come.
A: OK, thanks. That would be great. Is it a special occasion?
I: Well, my oldest sister has a new baby girl, so it's kind of a celebration for that.
A: Oh! So I should bring something then.
I: No, please don't. It isn't like that. There's no need.

J = Joanna, S = Sally
2

J: Hello, Sally. How are you?
S: Fine, thanks, Joanna. It's been a busy week.
J: Yes, I bet. How much longer are you in town for?
S: The conference ends tomorrow, and I'm leaving on Saturday.
J: Oh. Well, what are you doing tonight?
S: Nothing at the moment. I'll probably be in my hotel.
J: Would you like to come out for dinner? Let's go somewhere this evening.
S: Really? I'd love to.
J: Of course. I'd like to take you to my favorite restaurant.
S: That would be wonderful. I'd like that very much.
J: Great. Let's go right after work. I'll meet you downstairs in the lobby.
S: OK. What time?
J: I finish at six. Is that OK for you?
S: Sure. I'll see you then. Bye.

3A

COMBO
SPLIT

Life

SECOND EDITION

JOHN HUGHES
DAVID BOHLKE

Australia · Brazil · Mexico · Singapore · United Kingdom · United States

Contents

Unit 1	Lifestyle	page 4
Unit 2	Competitions	page 12
Unit 3	Transportation	page 20
Unit 4	Challenges	page 28
Unit 5	The environment	page 36
Unit 6	Stages of life	page 44
Audioscripts		page 100

Unit 1 Lifestyle

1a Global health

Grammar simple present

1 Complete the article about Nathan Wolfe with the simple present form of the verbs in parentheses.

How one scientist fights for global health

Nathan Wolfe is a scientist and he ¹ _____ (work) all over the world. He ² _____ (specialize) in viruses and diseases, and he often ³ _____ (go) to places with health problems. In particular, he ⁴ _____ (study) viruses and diseases from animals. It's an important job because he ⁵ _____ (want) to know how these viruses spread from animals to humans. As a result, Nathan ⁶ _____ (spend) a lot of time in regions with wildlife.

In the modern world, humans ⁷ _____ (not / stay) in one place anymore, so new viruses also ⁸ _____ (travel) more easily. When humans ⁹ _____ (visit) different regions, they ¹⁰ _____ (not / realize) how easy it is to bring a new kind of disease back with them.

However, the modern world with its technology also ¹¹ _____ (help) Nathan with his work. He often works in parts of the world where people ¹² _____ (not / have) electricity. A cell phone allows Nathan to continue his life-saving work.

virus (n) /vaiˈrəs/ a small living thing that enters a human body and makes you sick
disease (n) /dɪziːz/ an illness that affects humans and animals

---

▶ **SPELL CHECK simple present third person** *(he / she / it)* **verb endings**

We add -s to most verbs to form the simple present third person. However, note these exceptions:
- Add -es to verbs ending in -ch, -o, -s, -ss, -sh, and -x: *watch → watches*
- For verbs ending in -y after a consonant, change the -y to -i and add -es: *study → studies*
- *have* and *be* have irregular forms.

2 Look at the spell check box. Then write the simple present third-person form of these verbs.

1 start _____
2 match _____
3 fly _____
4 pass _____
5 live _____
6 try _____
7 finish _____
8 relax _____

3 Pronunciation /s/, /z/, or /ɪz/

▶ **01** Listen to the endings of these verbs. Write the verbs in the chart. Listen again and repeat.

goes	helps	realizes	specializes	spends	stays
studies	travels	visits	wants	works	

/s/	/z/	/ɪz/
_____	_____	_____
_____	_____	_____
_____	_____	
	_____	

4 Write questions about Nathan Wolfe and his work. Use the simple present.

1 (where / Nathan / work)

_____ ?

All over the world.

2 (where / he / often / go)

_____ ?

To places with health problems.

3 (what / he / study)

_____ ?

Viruses and diseases from animals.

4 (where / he / spend / a lot of time)

_____ ?

In regions with wildlife.

5 (why / new viruses / travel more easily)

_____ ?

Because humans travel all over the world.

6 (people / have electricity / in every part of the world)

_____

_____ ?

No, they don't.

7 (how / Nathan / communicate)

_____ ?

With a cell phone.

Listening healthy living quiz

5 ▶ 02 Look at the quiz. Then listen to a conversation between two people at work. Circle the speaker's answers (a–c).

Grammar adverbs of frequency

6 Put the words in the correct order to make sentences.

1 always / in the evening. / I / exercise

_____

_____

2 it / in the winter. / always / colder / is

_____

_____

3 take / twice a day. / I / this medicine

_____

_____

4 they / don't / go / often / on vacation.

_____

_____

5 on weekends. / we / sometimes / busy / are

_____

_____

6 eats out / rarely / she / during the week.

_____

_____

7 on time / are / never / for work. / you

_____

_____

Stress is bad for your health (both physical and mental)

Find out how stressed you are with this quick quiz.

1 I worry about money _____ .
   a every day   b at least once a week   c once a month

2 I _____ have problems sleeping at night.
   a never   b sometimes   c always

3 I _____ find it difficult to concentrate.
   a rarely   b sometimes   c often

4 Which of these sentences describes your lunchtimes?
   a I always eat lunch at my desk and reply to my emails.
   b I always eat lunch at my desk and read the newspaper or relax.
   c I always leave my desk, go for a walk, and eat my lunch somewhere else.

Reading community health

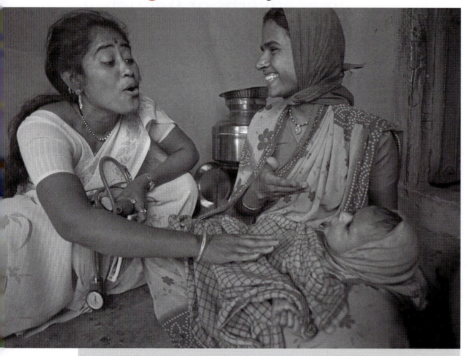

Mobile medicine

Sarubai Salve goes to work twice a day. She leaves her home once at 9:00 a.m. and then again at 6:00 p.m. to visit people in her village of Jawalke. The village has about 240 families and, with another woman named Babai Sathe, Sarubai is responsible for the villagers' health. The women visit pregnant women and give medicine to some of the older people. Today they are visiting their first patient. Rani Kale doesn't come from Jawalke. She lives about an hour away, but her village doesn't have anyone like Sarubai to help mothers-to-be. Sarubai is checking Rani and she is worried about the position of the baby. Rani might need to go to the hospital.

Half an hour later, Sarubai and Babai visit another mother with a three-month-old baby. While they are checking the baby, Sarubai gives the mother advice on healthy eating and vaccinations. Jawalke is a very different place because of the two women. They regularly deliver babies and continue to help as the child grows up. There is a shortage of doctors in this region, so village health workers are important because they can give medicine and advice.

A mobile team visits Jawalke once a week. The team includes a nurse and a doctor. The mobile team meets with Sarubai, and they look at any of her patients with serious medical problems. The health workers are an important connection between the mobile team and the local people. Currently there are 300 village health workers in the region, and the number is growing.

1 Read the article. Circle the correct option (a–c) to answer the questions.

1 How often does Sarubai visit people in the village?
   a once a day
   b twice a day
   c twice a week

2 How many doctors are there in the village of Jawalke?
   a one
   b two
   c none

3 Where does Rani Kale come from?
   a Jawalke
   b a village near Jawalke
   c we don't know

4 Sarubai meets Rani because she is
   _____ .
   a a new mother
   b pregnant
   c sick

5 Which of these statements is true about the health workers?
   a They only deliver babies.
   b They do the same job as doctors.
   c They have many different responsibilities.

6 What is the purpose of the mobile team?
   a to do the job of the health workers
   b to provide more medical help
   c to train the health workers

7 How do we know from the article that the village health project is successful?
   a because they are training more health workers
   b because patients say they are happy with their health workers
   c because the region doesn't need any more doctors

vaccination (n) /ˌvæksɪˈneɪʃ(ə)n/ medicine you put in the body to stop disease

2 Find words in the article for these definitions.

1 looks after (verb phrase) _____

2 when a woman is going to have a baby (adj) _____

3 a person with a medical problem who sees a doctor (n) _____

4 women who are going to have a baby (n) _____

5 a place for people with medical problems (n) _____

6 help a woman have a baby (v) _____

7 not enough of something (n) _____

8 can move from place to place (adj) _____

9 important and sometimes dangerous (adj) _____

10 near or in the same area (adj) _____

Grammar present continuous

3 Read the article again. Underline the four present continuous forms.

4 Circle the correct options to complete the sentences.

1 At the moment, *I drive / I'm driving* toward the city. Is this the right direction?

2 Where *do you come / are you coming* from originally?

3 Sorry, I can't hear you because a plane *flies / is flying* overhead.

4 *I never cycle / I'm never cycling* to work in the winter.

5 Someone *stands / is standing* at the front door. Can you see who it is?

6 *Do you always leave / Are you always leaving* for work this early in the morning?

7 It was warm earlier today, but now *it gets / it's getting* colder and colder.

8 *Do you work / Are you working* now, or *do you take / are you taking* a break?

5 Pronunciation contracted forms

▶ **03** Listen to the sentences. Write the number of words you hear in each sentence. Contracted forms (*I'm, we're, aren't, isn't*, etc.) count as one word.

a ___5___   d _____

b _____   e _____

c _____   f _____

▶ **SPELL CHECK** present continuous *-ing* endings

- With verbs ending in -e, delete the -e and add *-ing*: *dance* → *danc**ing***
- With verbs ending in -ie, delete the -e and change the *i* to a *y*: *die* → *dying*
- With some verbs ending in one vowel and a consonant, double the final consonant: *stop* → *stopping*

6 Look at the spell check box. Then write the *-ing* form of these verbs.

1 live _____   5 lie _____

2 drop _____   6 take _____

3 swim _____   7 get _____

4 have _____   8 jog _____

7 Dictation my typical day

▶ **04** The man in the photo below is describing his typical day. Listen and write the words you hear.

_____

_____

_____

_____

_____

_____

_____

_____

_____

_____

_____

1c A happy and healthy lifestyle

Listening an interview with Elizabeth Dunn

1 ▶ 05 Listen to an interview with Elizabeth Dunn. Complete the sentences.

1 Elizabeth is interested in what makes us feel _____ .

2 She does research on happiness and how _____ affects this.

3 As part of her research, she did an experiment with a group of _____ .

4 She thinks that experiences like visiting a new _____ are good for you.

2 ▶ 05 Listen again. Read these sentences and choose the correct option (a or b).

a Elizabeth agrees.
b Elizabeth disagrees.

1 Money is the most important thing. _____
2 Money doesn't make you feel happier. _____
3 Spending money on other people makes you happier. _____
4 Spending money on experiences makes you feel happy. _____

Word focus *feel*

3 Match the sentences (1–4) with the uses of *feel* (a–d).

1 I feel like going out for dinner tonight. ____
2 I don't feel this is the right thing to do. ____
3 I feel much happier today. ____
4 The sun feels warm. It felt a lot colder yesterday. ____

a talking about your emotions or health
b talking about an opinion
c talking about the weather
d talking about wanting to do something

4 Match the questions (1–4) with the answers (a–d).

1 How are you today? ____
2 What do you think about my work in general? ____
3 Do you feel like helping me with this? ____
4 What's the weather like? ____

a Actually, I feel you need to do more.
b It feels so cold outside!
c Sorry, I'm really busy at the moment.
d I'm feeling much better, thanks.

5 Write six different questions with the word *feel*. Use these words. You can use words more than once.

what	how do you
like	playing a game
OK	doing something
cold	

1 _____ ?
2 _____ ?
3 _____ ?
4 _____ ?
5 _____ ?
6 _____ ?

1d At the doctor's

Vocabulary medical problems

1 Complete the conversations with these words.

back	ear	head	mouth
nose	stomach	throat	tooth

1 A: Sorry, I have a really runny _____ today.
   B: It's OK. Here's a tissue if you need one.

2 A: I have a really bad _____ache.
   B: Is the problem in the left or the right one?

3 A: It's too painful to eat.
   B: It sounds like you have a _____ache. You should go to the dentist.

4 A: What's that noise?
   B: They're digging up the road outside.
   A: It's giving me a terrible _____ache.

5 A: I can hardly talk today.
   B: Why? Do you have a sore _____ ?

6 A: Can you pick this up for me? I have a bad _____ .
   B: Sure. But maybe you should lie down for a while.

7 A: My throat hurts, doctor.
   B: Well, let's have a look. Open your _____ , please.

8 A: What's the problem?
   B: I think I ate too much. I have a _____ache.

2 Pronunciation one or two syllables?

▶ **06** Listen to these sentences. Find the two-syllable words and underline the stressed syllable.

1 How does your <u>sto</u>mach feel?
2 Is your throat sore or is it better?
3 Drink this hot water.
4 Can I see the doctor about my ear?

Real life talking about illness

3 ▶ **07** Listen to a conversation at the doctor's. Check (✓) the correct options in the form and write the doctor's advice.

```
┌─────────────────────────────────────────────┐
│        Patient's medical problems             │
│                                               │
│ 1  Medical problem: sore throat ☐ headache ☐  │
│    stomachache ☐  earache ☐  cough ☐          │
│ 2  Temperature: low ☐  normal ☐  high ☐       │
│ 3  Details of prescription: medicine ☐ pills ☐ │
│ 4  Advice: _____  │
│    _____  │
└─────────────────────────────────────────────┘
```

4 ▶ **07** Complete the conversation with these phrases. Then listen again and check.

They are good	Do you have
~~How do you feel~~	If you still feel sick
not really	take this prescription
Let me have a	You need to
try drinking	Let me check

Doctor: ¹ _*How do you feel*_ today?
Patient: Not very well. I have a terrible sore throat.
Doctor: I see. ² _____ look. Open wide. Yes, it's very red in there.
Patient: I also have a bad cough.
Doctor: Do you have a stomachache?
Patient: No, ³ _____ .
Doctor: ⁴ _____ a temperature?
Patient: I don't think so. I don't feel hot.
Doctor: ⁵ _____ it … Yes, it's a little high. Do you have anything for it?
Patient: I bought some pills at the pharmacy, but they didn't do any good.
Doctor: Well, ⁶ _____ to the pharmacy. ⁷ _____ take some different pills. ⁸ _____ for your throat. Take one every four hours. You need to rest for a couple of days, and ⁹ _____ lots of water.
Patient: OK. Thank you.
Doctor: ¹⁰ _____ after a few days, come back and see me, but I think it's the flu.

> **prescription** (n) /prɪˈskrɪpʃən/ a piece of paper from the doctor with suggested medicine written on it. You give it to the pharmacist.
> **flu** (n) /fluː/ The flu gives people a fever and makes them feel sick.

5 Listen and respond giving advice

▶ **08** Listen to five friends with different medical problems. Respond with some advice. Then compare your advice with the model answer that follows.

> I have a headache.

> You need to take some pills.

1e Personal information

Writing filling out a form

1 Look at the medical form below. Find words and expressions in the form for these definitions (1–10).

1 What you put before your name ___Title___

2 The first letter of your middle name
_____

3 When you were born _____

4 Where to call you between 9 a.m. and 5 p.m. _____

5 How you feel overall _____

6 Times when you were very sick in the past
_____

7 How much exercise you do
_____

8 A person to call if there is a problem
_____

9 Numbers and letters at the end of your address _____

10 Your family name _____

Listening filling out a form

2 ▶ **09** Listen to a conversation at the doctor's. The receptionist is asking a new patient for personal information. Complete the medical form below with the information you hear.

3 **Writing skill information on forms**

Complete this information (1–12) with your own details.

1 Title _____

2 First name _____

3 Last name _____

4 Tel. no. _____

5 Occupation _____

6 Place of birth _____

7 DOB _____

8 Marital status _____

9 Gender _____

10 Nationality _____

11 No. of dependents _____

12 Contact person _____

Medical Details

Title _____ First Initial _____ Middle Initial _____

Last name _____ DOB _____

Address _____

_____

Zip code _____ Contact # (daytime) _____

General health _____

_____

Number of hours of exercise per week _____

Type of exercise/sports _____

Last visit to doctor _____

Previous serious illnesses _____

Contact person/number (in case of emergency) _____

Wordbuilding verb + noun collocations

1 Match the verbs in box A with the nouns in box B to make collocations. Then complete the sentences (1–7) with the collocations.

A	take	go	have	lift
	play	read	run	

B	a book	a coffee	the piano
	hiking	a marathon	
	weights	public transportation	

1 I'm training to _____ _____ next year. So far I can do about twenty kilometers.

2 I often _____ _____ in the mountains on weekends. It's very relaxing.

3 I _____ _____ when I have time. Mozart is my favorite composer.

4 Before I sleep at night, I usually _____ _____ . Fantasy or science fiction are my favorites.

5 I _____ _____ twice a week at the local gym. I'm getting stronger and stronger.

6 I _____ _____ to work instead of driving a car.

7 Can I _____ _____ with milk, please?

Learning skills recording new vocabulary

2 When you learn a new English word, how do you record it? Circle the information you record.

a the meaning
b the translation into your language
c the pronunciation
d the type of word (verb, adjective, noun, preposition, etc.)
e collocations
f phrases or expressions using this word

3 Which of these techniques do you use to help you remember new vocabulary?

a **Word groups**

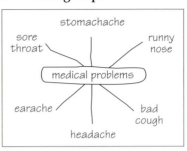

b **Drawings**

go hiking

c **Diagrams**

always often sometimes rarely never
100% ← _____ 50% _____ → 0%

4 Look at some of the new words from Unit 1.

1 Try recording some new information about the words. Use a dictionary to help you.

2 Try different techniques for learning the new words. Decide which techniques work well for you.

Check!

5 Complete the crossword. You can find the answers in Unit 1 of the Student Book.

Across

3 A large Italian island
6 You do this with plants and flowers
7 Measurement of how hot your body is
8 A person who lives to 100 years or more
10 A place to get medicine

Down

1 Give this to a friend if they have a problem
2 Something a doctor gives you for an illness
4 The speed of the heart
5 A Japanese island with some of the oldest people in the world
9 A short sleep

2a Paddleboard racing

Reading adventure sport

1 Read the article. Are these sentences true (T) or false (F)?

1 Paddleboarding is a combination of two water sports.   T   F

2 Competitive paddleboard races are usually on rivers.   T   F

3 The most important race is in the ocean around Hawaii.   T   F

4 Jamie Mitchell completed the Molokai to Oahu race in the fastest time.   T   F

5 The writer says paddleboard racing is a famous sport.   T   F

6 The prize money for first place in the race is three thousand dollars.   T   F

7 Jamie is a full-time professional athlete.   T   F

Paddleboard racing

Paddleboarding is a mixture of two water sports— surfing and rowing. Paddleboarding uses a surfboard, and the paddleboarder "rows" the board. However, there are two big differences. In surfing, you have to stand, but in paddleboarding you can kneel or lie on the board. In rowing you use oars, but in paddleboarding you can't use oars. You have to use your arms to move along. Competitors must be strong and athletic.

You can do the sport on rivers, but most competitions are on the ocean. The main competition for paddleboarders is the annual race from Molokai to Oahu in Hawaii, a distance of 50 kilometers. On a good day, with the right kind of waves, you don't always have to use your arms because the water carries you some of the way. However, on a bad day, you have to use your arms the whole way.

One of paddleboarding's most famous competitors is the Australian Jamie Mitchell, an eight-time winner of the Molokai to Oahu race. He also holds the record time of four hours, fifty-eight minutes, and twenty-five seconds.

Because the sport isn't well known, the prize money for winning paddleboarding is small—Mitchell only received $3,000 for winning the race this year. But Mitchell obviously loves the sport because he trains two or three times a day, six days a week, for the four months before the race. At the same time, he has to earn money, so he does anything including working in bars or construction work.

So how does Mitchell stay interested in such a sport? He says, "I just love paddleboarding. It's not about winning. It's about coming to Hawaii and spending time with my good friends in a place that I love."

2 Match these words from the article with the definitions (1–6).

athletic	kneel	oars	rowing	surfing	waves

1 sport of riding waves on the sea (n) _____

2 sport of moving a boat through water with oars (n) _____

3 put both knees on a flat surface (v) _____

4 long pieces of wooden equipment used to row a boat (n) _____

5 water on the sea that goes up and down (n) _____

6 physically strong and good at sports (adj) _____

Grammar modal verbs for rules

3 Rewrite these sentences using a form of *can*, *have to*, or *must*. Sometimes more than one answer is possible. Then compare your answers to the sentences in the article.

1 In surfing, it's necessary to stand on your board.
   In surfing, you *have to / must* stand on your board.

2 Paddleboarders are allowed to kneel or lie on the board.
   Paddleboarders _____ kneel or lie on the board.

3 In paddleboarding, you are not allowed to use oars.
   In paddleboarding, you _____ use oars.

4 It's necessary to use your arms to move along.
   You _____ use your arms to move along.

5 Paddleboarders are allowed to practice on rivers.
   Paddleboarders _____ practice on rivers.

4 Pronunciation *n't*

▶ **10** Listen and circle the form you hear. Then listen again and repeat.

1 They *do / don't* have to win.

2 He *can / can't* win the game.

3 *Do / Don't* you have to wear a helmet?

4 A player *can / can't* hit the ball twice.

5 Write one rule for each sport (1–4). Use words from boxes A, B, and C.

A Each team	The ball	The referee	You

B has to / must	can	don't have to

C send a player off the field.
go over the net.
have five players on the court.
use any special equipment.

1 Basketball: *Each team has to / must have five players on the court.*

2 Soccer: _____

_____

3 Running: _____

_____

4 Tennis: _____

_____

Vocabulary sports

6 Complete the sentences with one word. The first letter is provided.

1 She's taking part in a r_____ to the top of the mountain.

2 W_____ at the Olympics get a gold medal because they beat all the other competitors.

3 They scored 14 p_____ in the first quarter.

4 The two runners crossed the finish l_____ at the same time, so they both came in first.

5 The r_____ gave out two red cards and six yellow cards during the match.

6 A: Which is your favorite t_____ ?
   B: The one in red.

7 Can you explain the r_____ of American football? I don't understand the sport.

8 There were 48,000 s_____ at the soccer match.

2b Sports and leisure activities

Reading walking soccer

1 Read the article. Answer the questions (1–7) with words from the article.

1 Do more people watch the World Cup or the Olympic Games on TV? _____

2 Which types of teams play soccer every weekend? _____

3 How old are the players in walking soccer? _____

4 What are the health benefits of walking soccer? _____

5 Which two rules are different from normal soccer? _____ _____

6 Why don't many people watch walking soccer? _____

7 How many teams play walking soccer in the United Kingdom now? _____

2 Vocabulary extra talking about likes and dislikes

a Match the highlighted verbs in the speech bubbles with the emoticons (a–f).

> I enjoy swimming when I have time.

> I love winning!

> I really like watching sports on TV.

> I hate boxing.

> I can't stand losing!

> I don't mind playing baseball, but I don't like watching it.

a ☺☺☺ _____
b ☺☺ _____
c ☺ like, _____
d 😐 _____
e ☹ dislike, _____
f ☹☹ _____ , _____

b Complete the sentences so they are true for you.

1 I love playing _____ .
2 I enjoy _____ when I have time.
3 I don't mind _____ .
4 I don't like watching _____ on TV.
5 I can't stand _____ .

Walking soccer

Globally, more people play soccer than any other sport, and more people watch the World Cup on TV than the Olympic Games. Every weekend, thousands of teams meet in different countries to compete against each other. That includes famous teams such as Real Madrid and Manchester United, and local teams of people playing competitively or just for fun. From an early age, schoolchildren play soccer in their physical education classes and compete against teams from other schools. Now, a new type of soccer is growing in popularity. It's called "walking soccer."

Most soccer players retire from competitive games in their 30s, but walking soccer is for people over 50. It's a great way to keep fit and it can help older people live longer. Doctors also say it's good for the mind. Most walking soccer matches are informal and social. Most of the rules are the same as for normal soccer, but everything is much slower. Players have to walk with the ball—they can't run. Also, players have to keep one foot on the ground at all times, so they can't jump.

Not surprisingly, walking soccer doesn't get many spectators because it is very slow. But more and more people like playing it. For example, in the United Kingdom, there were around 100 teams two years ago. Now there are over 800, with regular competitions in different parts of the country every year.

Grammar *-ing* form

3 Complete the sentences with the *-ing* form of these verbs.

| join | become | watch | cycle | fly |
| learn | lose | ~~play~~ | sit | |

1 *Playing* tennis is fun and it's very good for your health.
2 We love _____ because you get fit and watch the countryside go by at the same time.
3 _____ to play the piano takes years of practice.
4 I'm very competitive. When I play games, I don't like _____ . I get really angry.
5 _____ in front of the TV all day isn't good for you.
6 Are you interested in _____ our team? We still have some spots available.
7 I don't like traveling by plane because I'm afraid of _____ .
8 Have you ever thought of _____ a professional athlete in the future?
9 You play golf every week, so why do you hate _____ it on TV?

4 Pronunciation /ŋ/

a ▶ **11** Listen to these words. Underline the part of the word with the /ŋ/ sound.

1 watching
2 language
3 waiting
4 thinks
5 cycling
6 losing
7 winning
8 English
9 competing
10 thanks

b ▶ **11** Listen again and repeat the words.

5 Dictation Kristi Leskinen

▶ **12** Listen to part of a documentary about the skier Kristi Leskinen. Complete the text with the words you hear.

Kristi Leskinen is a famous skier. She [1] _____ _____,
but her favorite place is Mammoth Mountain in the USA. [2]_____
such as kayaking, but she [3]_____
_____ .
Recently, she was in a TV show called *The Superstars*. In the show, famous [4]_____
_____
that [5]_____ .
Kristi won [6]_____ .
But now it's winter again, so she needs to go back to the mountains and start training. This year,
[7]_____

a lot more medals.

2c Dangerous sports

Listening *free diving*

1 ▶ 13 Listen to a sports program about Annelie Pompe, a free diver. Number the topics (a–d) in the order the presenter talks about them (1–4).

 —— a when Annelie climbed Mount Everest
 —— b a definition of free diving
 —— c why Annelie likes free diving
 —— d why Annelie likes doing other sports

2 ▶ 13 Listen again. Circle the correct option (a–c) to complete each sentence.

1 Free diving is an underwater sport in which the diver _____ use breathing equipment.
 a has to b doesn't have to c can't

2 Annelie's world record is a dive of _____ meters.
 a 120 b 126 c 136

3 Annelie spends every _____ training in the sea.
 a morning b afternoon c weekend

4 Annelie _____ other sports.
 a likes doing
 b doesn't have time for
 c doesn't like doing

5 For Annelie, adventure is about going to the _____ parts of the world.
 a deepest
 b highest
 c deepest and highest

Word focus *like*

3 Match the sentences (1–7) with the different uses of *like* (a–g).

1 He's like his older brother. He was good at sports, too. _____
2 He looks like his older brother. He has black hair, too. _____
3 I'd like to win a gold medal one day. _____
4 I'd like a cup of coffee, please. _____
5 Do you feel like going out later? _____
6 I like most sports. _____
7 I like watching most sports. _____

a to talk about things you enjoy (*like* + noun)
b to talk about activities you enjoy doing (*like* + *-ing*)
c use with *would* to say you want to do something (*would like to* + base verb)
d use with *would* to say you want something (*would like* + noun)
e to describe behavior similar to something or someone
f used with the verbs *look, smell, sound,* and *taste* to describe similarities with someone or something (*look like*, etc.)
g use with *feel* to talk about wanting to do something (*feel like* + *-ing*)

4 Rewrite the sentences (1–5) using the word *like*.

1 They want to play tennis later.
 They *'d like to play tennis later* . OR
 They *feel like playing tennis later* .

2 You're very similar in appearance to someone I went to school with.
 You _____ I went to school with.

3 She wants to play tennis professionally someday.
 She _____ tennis professionally someday.

4 We want some ice cream, please.
 We _____ , please.

5 He isn't similar to his sister. She always worked very hard.
 He _____ his sister. She always worked very hard.

2d Joining a group

Reading leaflet for fitness classes

1 Read the leaflet for fitness classes at a local gym. Match the sentences (1–6) with the classes (A–C).

1 You have to get up early for this class. _____
2 The person in charge tells you what to do. _____
3 This class is good after a day at work. _____
4 This class mixes enjoyment with exercise. _____
5 Take a break from work and come exercise. _____
6 You will notice a difference very quickly. _____

Fit for Life Gym

A

◀ Boot Camp starts at 6 a.m. every morning with your instructor. He shouts orders and you run, jump, lift. It's non-stop exercise for 90 minutes.

"Perfect for people who want fast results."

Our evening Pilates classes help your body recover after a hard day at work. Build strength with an exercise program suitable for any age and fitness level. ▶ **B**

"After a day in the office chair, Pilates is perfect for your muscles."

C

◀ Our Zumba classes are a mixture of fun, excitement, and high energy levels. Classes are at midday, so you can even join us during your lunch break.

"Zumba is a fun way to get fit— every class feels like a party!"

Real life talking about interests

2 ▶ **14** Listen to two friends talking about the leaflet. Number the fitness classes in the order they discuss them (1–3).

Boot Camp _____   Pilates _____   Zumba _____

3 ▶ **14** Listen again. Complete the conversation with the words you hear.

A: Hey, this looks interesting.
B: What?
A: This leaflet for fitness classes at the gym. Are you [1] _____ _____ doing something like that?
B: Maybe. But I'm [2] _____ _____ good at sports.
A: But this isn't competitive. It's for getting fit. This one [3] _____ _____ : Boot Camp. What about joining that?
B: What is Boot Camp?
A: It's like the army. You have someone who tells you what to do. I think [4] _____ _____ do it. It starts at six o'clock.
B: Great. So we can go after work.
A: No, it's six in the morning.
B: What?! I hate getting up early. [5] _____ _____ doing something that starts later?
A: Well, there's one at lunchtime. It's called Zumba. It's a kind of dance class, I think.
B: I [6] _____ _____ dancing.
A: Really? It looks pretty fun.
B: What about something after work?
A: There's a Pilates class. It doesn't give an exact time, but it says it's after work.
B: Well, [7] _____ _____ that to Boot Camp or dancing.
A: Yes, [8] _____ _____ good.

4 **Listen and respond** saying what you are interested in doing

▶ **15** A friend wants you to join one of the classes in Exercise 1. You are only interested in Pilates. Listen to your friend and respond each time. Then compare your responses with the model answers that follow.

> Are you interested in Boot Camp?

> No, I wouldn't like to do it.

2e Advertising an event

Writing an ad or notice

1 Imagine you are organizing a social event for everyone after work. Write a notice for everyone and tell them:

- it's a barbecue in the local park with a fun soccer match afterward.
- the date and time.
- the reason (it's a way for everyone to meet each other).
- your email address (so they can say if they are coming).

_____

_____

_____

_____

_____

_____

_____

_____

2 Grammar extra punctuation rules

Complete the rules for punctuation (1–4) with these words.

apostrophe	capital letter
comma	exclamation mark
period	

1 You have to use a _____ when it's the first word of a sentence; with names of people, places, and countries; with days of the week and months; and with people's titles.

2 You must end a sentence with a _____ , or you can emphasize something with an _____ .

3 A _____ can separate lists of nouns or adjectives, and sometimes two clauses.

4 You have to use an _____ with contracted forms and with the possessive 's.

3 Writing skill checking and correcting your writing

Read "My free time" written by a student. Three lines are correct, and seven lines have mistakes. Check (✓) the correct lines and correct the other lines.

<u>My free time</u>

Ⓘhave many different hobbies
and interests such as computer
gaming cycling, and painting, but
my favorite is ice hockey. Its a
very popular sport in my home
country of canada. I practice
every saturday morning at our
local sports center with my team,
and we play matches once a month
We love to win

1 *I (capital letter)* _____
2 ✓ _____
3 _____
4 _____
5 _____
6 _____
7 _____
8 _____
9 _____
10 _____

Wordbuilding suffixes

1 Complete the words for the people shown in these pictures.

1 golf_____

2 cycl_____

3 swim_____

4 race car driv_____

5 javelin throw_____

6 run_____

Learning skills using a dictionary (1)

2 Match the different parts of the dictionary entries (1–12) with these words.

adjective	_____	definition	_____
example sentence	_____	first meaning	_____
main stress	_____	noun	_____
past participle	_____	plural form	_____
present participle	_____	pronunciation	_____
second meaning	_____	verb	_____

---

compete /kəmˈpiːt/ (v) (competing, competed) [1] take part in a contest or game. *Ten people competed in the race.* [2] try to get something for yourself and stop others from getting it. *My company is competing with another company for an important customer.*

competition /ˌkɒmpˈtɪʃən/ (n) (competitions) [1] an event when two or more people take part in a contest or game to find the best at the activity. *Lucy won the school's writing competition.* [2] when two or more people are trying to get something and stop others from getting it. *There's a lot of competition for the trophy.*

competitive /ˌkəmpeˈtɪtɪv/ (adj) [1] of situations or events when people compete with each other. *Professional tennis is a very competitive sport.* [2] of a person who wants to be the best at something. *I'm a very competitive person who loves winning!*

Check!

3 Complete the sentences with these numbers. You can find the answers in Unit 2 of the Student Book.

1.50	2	4	5	18	60	180

1 In the Ironman competition, you have to cycle _____ kilometers.

2 You must be over _____ years old to enter the World Beard and Moustache Championships.

3 A Mud Bowl match lasts _____ minutes.

4 Esperanza pays $ _____ to watch the wrestling.

5 There are _____ syllables in *competition*.

6 At the annual Idiotarod race, there are _____ people in a team.

7 The match was a draw. The score was 2 – _____ .

3a Choosing greener transportation

Reading green transportation

1 Read the article. What is the aim of the article? Circle the correct option (a–c).

a to give an opinion about transportation
b to argue for more public transportation
c to give information about a new type of transportation

2 Read the article again. Are these sentences true (T) or false (F), according to the information in the article?

1 The author thinks walking is better than driving when you visit a city.   T   F

2 Renting bicycles from hotels and hostels can be very expensive.   T   F

3 The author thinks most cities need to give more information to visitors.   T   F

4 Buses, trains, and ferries are better for the environment than cars or airplanes.   T   F

Vocabulary transportation nouns

3 Match the words in box A with the words in box B to make compound nouns. Then complete the sentences with the compound nouns.

A	fuel	public	rush	speed	traffic

B	hour	jam	limit	costs	transportation

1 _____ _____ begins around 8 a.m. and ends at around 9 a.m. in my city.

2 There's a _____ _____ all the way from downtown to the airport. Nothing is moving.

3 It's really expensive to have a car. _____ _____ go up every year!

4 My city has excellent _____ _____ . There are frequent buses and trains.

5 Cameras can catch people driving over the _____ _____ .

Choosing greener transportation

For tourists and travelers who want a more interesting experience when they arrive in a new city or country, here are some better ways to travel, both for you and for the environment.

Step 1 Get out of the car and walk. It's slower, but it's the greenest way to travel. It's also the most rewarding way to see a city, but remember to pack comfortable shoes.

Step 2 Cycling is also a good alternative. Many hotels and hostels now offer free bicycles for guests. Some cities also have bike stations. You pick up a bicycle from one of these stations and return it after two hours. It's not free, but it's much cheaper than a bus or taxi.

Step 3 If you have to take transportation in a city, take public transportation. Most cities now offer lots of information and very clear maps. You'll also get more detailed information by visiting the city website before you go.

Step 4 Whenever possible, take buses, trains, or ferries for traveling. They are usually greener than cars and airplanes.

Step 5 And when the only way to travel is by car, rent a hybrid or electric car. Many car rental companies now offer this kind of choice, so always ask. Look for hotels at your destination with free electric vehicle charging stations. You'll be surprised how many hotels now offer this facility.

Grammar comparatives and superlatives

4 Look at the article again. Underline the examples of comparative and superlative forms.

> ▶ **SPELL CHECK comparatives and superlatives**
> - Add *-er* or *-est* to short adjectives: *young – younger – youngest*
> - When the adjectives end in *-e*, add *-r* or *-st*: *large – larger – largest*
> - Change adjectives ending in *-y* (after a consonant) to *-i* and add *-er* or *-est*: *happy – happier – happiest*
> - Double the final consonant of adjectives ending with a consonant + vowel + consonant: *hot – hotter – hottest*
> - Don't double the final consonant for adjectives ending in vowel + *-w* or *-y*: *slow – slower – slowest*

5 Look at the spell check box. Then write the comparative and superlative forms of these adjectives.

1	cheap	*cheaper*	*cheapest*
2	angry	_____	_____
3	large	_____	_____
4	big	_____	_____
5	safe	_____	_____
6	funny	_____	_____
7	thin	_____	_____
8	low	_____	_____
9	easy	_____	_____
10	green	_____	_____

6 Write sentences that give your opinion. Use a comparative form of the adjectives in parentheses.

1 traveling by bus / traveling by car (relaxing)
   I think *traveling by bus is more relaxing than traveling by car.*

2 cake / bread (sweet)
   I think _____

3 email / letters (fast)
   I think _____

4 trains / airplanes (bad for the environment)
   I think _____

7 Complete the text about transportation world records with the superlative forms of these adjectives.

dangerous	fast	long	small	tall

WORLD RECORDS TRANSPORTATION

- Gregory Dunham built the world's ¹ _____ rideable motorbike. It's 3.429 meters high.
- The ² _____ jet aircraft in the world is only 3.7 meters long and 5.7 meters wide (including wings).
- Marek Turowski drove the world's ³ _____ motorized sofa! The piece of furniture traveled at a speed of 148 kilometers per hour.
- Emil and Liliana Schmid took the ⁴ _____ journey ever. They drove 641,115 kilometers—and they are still driving!
- Billy Baxter broke the record for the fastest speed on a motorbike without seeing. He wore a blindfold over his eyes and reached 265.33 kilometers per hour. So it was probably one of the ⁵ _____ journeys ever as well.

8 Pronunciation sentence stress in comparative and superlative sentences

▶ **16** Listen to these sentences and underline the stressed words. Then listen again and repeat.

1 Your car is faster than mine.
2 Bicycles are the greenest transportation.
3 Walking is slower than cycling.
4 Hybrid transportation is the most efficient.

3b World transportation

Reading beautiful animals

1 Read the article about camels. Answer the questions.

1 What are camels famous for?

_____
_____

2 In what ways are camels useful to humans?

_____

3 Does everyone agree that camels are beautiful?

_____

4 How long does the competition last?

_____

5 How many camels enter the competition?

_____

6 What do the family and friends eat at the party?

_____

Grammar *as ... as*

2 Put the words in the correct order to make sentences. Start with the words in **bold**.

1 cars / in the forest / good as / **Horses** / are as

_____

2 isn't always / as this / **The weather** / as hot

_____
_____

3 expensive / **Silver** / isn't / as / as gold

_____

4 as cars / from / aren't / the sixties / **New cars** / stylish / as

_____

5 **Bicycles** / as / cars / are / in the city center / as fast

_____
_____

6 as I / used / not as / to be / **I'm** / young

_____
_____

3 Pronunciation /əz/

▶ **17** /əz/ is the sound of *as* in sentences with *as ... as*. Listen to the sentences in Exercise 2 and repeat them using this sound.

Beauty competitions for camels

Camels are famous for their ability to travel through the hot desert with heavy loads. But people don't only use them for transportation. Camels also produce milk to drink and meat to eat. So everyone agrees that they are useful animals—but how many of us would describe camels as beautiful? Camels have a large hump, strange knees, skinny legs, and ugly teeth. They are NOT beautiful. But not everyone agrees.

Once a year, people bring their camels from Oman, Saudi Arabia, Qatar, and even further away, to an area of land in Abu Dhabi. They come here to find the most beautiful camel. The competition lasts ten days. There are around 24,000 camels in the competition. The winning camel must have good ears, a high back, shiny hair, a long neck, and long legs. There is a prize for the winner, but this isn't as important as family honor.

This year, the winner was a man named Bin Tanaf. Immediately, his family and friends began to celebrate, and the party at his tent lasted all night. Two hundred people were there. They sang songs and told stories about camels. Everyone ate a lot of food, including rice and meat. In the middle of the celebration, a man brought a large plate into the tent. There was a large piece of yellow meat on it. "Ah," said Bin Tanaf, "The hump."

hump (n) / hʌmp / the top of the camel's back
honor (n) / ˈɑːnər / respect for someone who does something important

Word focus *as*

4 You can use *as* in different ways. Match the sentences (1–4) with the uses of *as* (a–d).

1 As we're late, let's take a taxi. _____
2 That car looks as if it's very old. _____
3 Traveling to Boston by train is as fast as traveling by plane. _____
4 As we drove past a field, we saw a horse. _____

a to compare two things
b to talk about appearance
c to talk about two actions happening at the same time
d to talk about the reason for something

5 Rewrite the sentences (1–4) using *as*.

1 We were late because there was a traffic jam.

   We were late _____

   _____ .

2 You look like you had a long journey.

   _____ if you had a long journey.

3 In the city, the speed of a bicycle is the same as the speed of a bus.

   In the city, _____ fast as a bus.

4 We saw an elephant when we drove home!

   We saw an elephant _____ !

Vocabulary transportation adjectives

6 Read the conversation between two friends visiting London. Replace the words in **bold** with these adjectives.

convenient	comfortable	frequent
traditional	punctual	reliable

A: Let's get a bus to Oxford Street. My guidebook says they are [1]**regular** and [2]**always on time**. There's one coming this way.
B: But it doesn't say "Oxford Street" on the front. Can we get a black cab? They are very [3]**old**.
A: But it'll be expensive!
B: But it's [4]**easy**. Buses are never [5]**there when you need them**. Look! This taxi's stopping.
A: Wow! This is so [6]**nice to sit in**!

1 _____   4 _____
2 _____   5 _____
3 _____   6 _____

Grammar comparative modifiers

7 Read the information about transportation in four countries. Then circle the correct options to complete the sentences.

	CARS	MOTORBIKES	BICYCLES
France	83%	12%	59%
South Korea	84%	9%	63%
Brazil	47%	29%	53%
South Africa	31%	7%	16%

1 The percentage of people with a car is *a bit / a lot* lower in France than in South Korea.
2 Cars are *much / a little* more popular than motorbikes in France.
3 The percentage of people with bicycles in South Korea is *a little / much* higher than in France.
4 In South Korea, bicycles are *a bit / a lot* more popular than motorbikes.
5 Cars are *a lot / a bit* less popular in South Africa than in France.
6 The percentage of people with bicycles in South Africa is *much / a little* lower than in Brazil.
7 In South Africa, motorbikes are *much / a bit* less popular than in South Korea.

	CARS	MOTORBIKES	BICYCLES
Italy	89%	26%	63%
Indonesia	4%	8%	65%
Malaysia	82%	83%	53%

8 Look at the information for three more countries and complete the sentences. Use a modifier and the comparative form of the adjective in parentheses.

1 The percentage of people with a car is _____ in Italy than in Indonesia. (high)
2 Bicycles are _____ than motorbikes in Italy. (popular)
3 The percentage of people with bicycles in Malaysia is _____ than in Indonesia. (low)
4 In Malaysia, cars are _____ than motorbikes. (popular)

3c Transportation in India

Listening the Golden Quadrilateral

1 ▶ **18** Listen to a documentary about a new road in India called the Golden Quadrilateral (GQ). Number the topics (a–d) in the order the presenter talks about them (1–4).

_____ a transportation and industry on the GQ
_____ b how the GQ will help the economy
_____ c the length and technology of the GQ
_____ d people in India are buying more and
          more cars

poverty (n) /ˈpɒvərti/ a situation where people are poor and do not have money to pay for basic things
highway (n) /ˈhaɪweɪ/ a large road with many lanes
symbol (n) /ˈsɪmb(ə)l/ something or someone that represents an idea

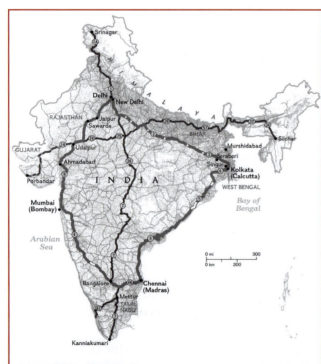

2 ▶ **18** Listen again and answer the questions. Circle the correct answer (a–c).

1 How many new cars every year will people in India probably buy in the next few years?
   a 1.5 million
   b two million
   c three million

2 Where do many of the rich people in India live?
   a next to the new road
   b in the cities
   c in the countryside

3 How long is the new road?
   a 600 kilometers
   b 6,000 kilometers
   c 60,000 kilometers

4 What types of transportation can you see on the new road?
   a all types
   b mostly cars
   c the presenter doesn't say

5 Why does the presenter describe the new road as "a symbol of India's future"?
   a because it's the same shape as the country of India
   b because it is helping the economy grow
   c because many people in India own cars

Vocabulary transportation verbs

3 Cross out the verb that does NOT fit in each group of collocations (1–6).

1 _catch / miss / ~~pick up~~_   a train
2 _drop off / catch / pick up_   a passenger
3 _catch / go by / get on_   a flight
4 _drop off / get in / take_   a taxi
5 _ride / get off / go in_   a bicycle
6 _take / miss / go_   a bus

4 **Pronunciation** /æ/ or /eɪ/

▶ **19** Match these words with the vowel sounds /æ/ or /eɪ/. Then listen, check, and repeat.

catch	change	day	gate	jam	plan
plane	stand	take	taxi	train	

/æ/ _____
/eɪ/ _____

3d Getting around town

Vocabulary taking transportation

1 Complete the sentences (1–8) with these words.

book	check in	fare	gate
platform	receipt	stand	stop

1 How much is the bus _____ to the airport?
2 There's a taxi _____ by the station, so you can get one there.
3 Is there a bus _____ near here?
4 Would you like a _____ for your purchase?
5 Flight AA 387 leaves from _____ 29.
6 The train to Atlanta is arriving at _____ 3.
7 Where do I go to _____ for my flight?
8 It's often cheaper to _____ your ticket online.

Real life going on a trip

2 ▶ **20** Listen to four conversations. Match the conversations (1–4) with the type of transportation (a–d).

a taxi _____   b bus _____
c train _____   d plane _____

3 ▶ **20** Listen again and answer the questions.

Conversation 1
1 Does the bus stop near the movie theater?
_____
2 What kind of ticket does he buy?
_____

Conversation 2
3 How much is a first-class ticket to the city?
_____
4 Which platform does it leave from?
_____

Conversation 3
5 How much does an extra bag cost?
_____
6 Can she pay by credit card?
_____

Conversation 4
7 Why can't the taxi stop where the person wants?
_____
8 How much is the taxi fare?
_____

4 ▶ **20** Complete the four conversations with these phrases. Then listen again and check.

Can I have	Can I pay	Do you go
Here you go	How many	How much
I'd like a	Which platform	

Conversation 1
A: Hi. [1] _____ downtown?
B: Which part?
A: Near the movie theater.
B: Yes, we stop in front of it.
A: Great. [2] _____ a round-trip ticket, please?

Conversation 2
A: [3] _____ first-class ticket to the city, please.
B: That's forty-two dollars.
A: Here you are. [4] _____ is it?
B: Platform 12.

Conversation 3
A: [5] _____ bags are you checking in?
B: Two.
A: I'm afraid your ticket only includes one bag. You'll have to pay an extra $20 for that one.
B: Oh, OK. [6] _____ by credit card?
A: Sure.

Conversation 4
A: It's just up here on the right. You can drop me off over there.
B: I can't stop there. It's a bus stop. But here is fine.
A: OK. [7] _____ is that?
B: That's $13.30.
A: [8] _____ .

5 Listen and respond responding to questions about travel

▶ **21** Listen to five questions about travel. Respond to each question with a phrase from the box. Then compare your response with the model answer that follows.

Round-trip, please.	No, with cash.
Platform 9.	Yes, this one.
Yes, I do. Here you are.	

What kind of train ticket would you like?

Round-trip, please.

3e Quick communication

1 Dictation telephone messages

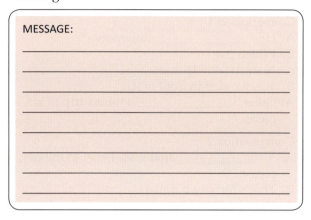**22** Listen to three cell phone messages. Write every word you hear in each message.

Message 1

```
MESSAGE:
_____
_____
_____
_____
_____
```

Message 2

```
MESSAGE:
_____
_____
_____
_____
_____
```

Message 3

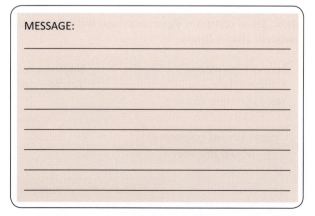

```
MESSAGE:
_____
_____
_____
_____
_____
```

Writing notes and messages

2 Look at the messages you wrote in Exercise 1. Rewrite them in note form. Remember to leave out words like articles, pronouns, auxiliary verbs, and polite forms.

Message 1

```
MESSAGE:
_____
_____
_____
```

Message 2

```
MESSAGE:
_____
_____
_____
```

Message 3

```
MESSAGE:
_____
_____
_____
_____
```

Wordbuilding compound nouns

1 Look at the wordbuilding box. Then complete the compound nouns in the sentences (1–6) with these words.

transportation	credit	driver
time	center	seat

1 Sorry, we don't accept _____ cards, only cash.
2 He works at night, so he usually sleeps in the day_____ .
3 There is road construction in the city _____ , so you shouldn't drive to the theater this evening.
4 I know I should take public _____ , but it's easier to drive my own car.
5 Do you have any change to pay the taxi _____ ?
6 I always book a window _____ when I travel by plane.

2 Match the words in box A with the words in box B to make compound nouns.

A	alarm	bank	boxing	cell
	soccer	tennis	city	mail

B	account	box	hall	clock
	field	gloves	phone	court

1   *alarm clock*
2 _____
3 _____
4 _____
5 _____
6 _____
7 _____
8 _____

Learning skills remembering new vocabulary

3 Look at the list of ways to remember new vocabulary. Check (✓) the ones you use now, and put an asterisk (*) by the ones you would like to use in the future.

Ways to remember new vocabulary

1 After I finish a unit in the Student Book, I read it again a few weeks later. ◯

2 When I find a new word or expression in the unit, I highlight it. ◯

3 I write a new word on a piece of paper. On the other side of the paper, I write a definition. Then I test myself. ◯

4 When I learn a new word, I check in my dictionary for other word forms, e.g., *commute* (v), *commuter* (n). ◯

5 I write new words in lists. Then I cover the words and try to translate them from my own language. ◯

6 I write the new word in a sentence that is important to me. ◯

7 I read more texts on similar subjects to the unit. I usually find some of the new words in the text. ◯

8 I choose ten new words and write a short story using them all. ◯

4 Do you use other techniques for learning and remembering vocabulary? Write them down and compare your ideas with other students in your next lesson.

Check!

5 Put the letters in the correct order to make words from Unit 3 in the Student Book.

1 LUANPCTU (meaning "on time") _____
2 LAKATOK (a city in India) _____
3 RODIDTIA (a famous dog race) _____
4 DASTN (where taxis stop and wait) _____
5 SSPAORTP (an official travel document) _____
6 JETACDIVE (type of word between *as* and *as*) _____

Unit 4 Challenges

4a Challenges and adventures

1 Vocabulary extra adventure

Replace the words in **bold** with these similar words or phrases.

adventure	ambition	a big challenge	take risks
crazy		dangerous	my biggest achievement

1 I don't like to **do things that could be dangerous**. _____
2 My life is so boring. I want a life of **doing exciting things**. _____
3 Don't walk so close to the cliff. It looks **unsafe**. _____
4 Getting straight A's at college has been **the thing that needed the most hard work and effort** in my life so far.

   _____
5 Climbing Mount Everest presents mountaineers with **something that is really difficult to do**, but that's what makes it worth doing!

   _____
6 As I get older, I have less and less **I want to achieve**. _____
7 It's snowing outside. We can't walk a hundred kilometers in this weather! Are you completely **mad**? _____

Grammar simple past

2 Look at the spell check box. Then write the simple past form of these regular verbs (1–8).

> ▶ **SPELL CHECK simple past regular verbs (-ed endings)**
>
> - Add -ed to verbs ending in a consonant: *watch → watched*
> - Add -d to verbs ending in -e: *dance → danced*
> - With verbs ending in -y (after a consonant), change the y to i and add -ed: *cry → cried*
> - Don't change the -y to -i after a vowel: *play → played*
> - Double the final consonant for most verbs ending in consonant + vowel + consonant: *stop → stopped*

1 visit _____   5 jog _____
2 arrive _____   6 live _____
3 dry _____   7 study _____
4 stay _____   8 move _____

3 Complete the paragraphs below and on page 29 with the simple past form of these verbs.

The TV presenter

~~be born~~	become	go	start	study	survive

The circus performer

grow up	join	learn	play

The TV presenter

Brady Barr [1] *was born* in 1963. He [2] _____ Science Education at university and then he [3] _____ a teacher. However, a few years later, he [4] _____ on a scientific expedition to learn more about crocodiles. He joined *National Geographic* TV in 1997 and [5] _____ presenting TV shows about dangerous animals. Recently, a three-and-a-half meter python attacked Brady during filming. Luckily, Brady [6] _____ .

python (n) /ˈpaɪθɑːn/ a large, dangerous snake

The circus performer

Eskil Ronningsbakken [7] _____ in Norway. As a child, he enjoyed climbing trees and he [8] _____ on the roofs of houses. He [9] _____ to do a handstand when he was five, and he studied circus skills when he was eight. At age 17, he [10] _____ a circus, but two years later he started performing on his own with his balancing act.

4 Read the paragraphs again. Are these sentences true (T) or false (F)? Rewrite the false sentences to make them correct.

1   Brady was born in 1975.
    F – Brady was born in 1963.

2   Brady joined a TV channel in 1997.
    _____

3   Brady attacked a python on his TV show.
    _____

4   Eskil was interested in the circus when he was a child.
    _____

5   Eskil joined a theater when he was seventeen.
    _____

6   Eskil started performing with a group of people after he left the circus.
    _____

5 A journalist asked Brady and Eskil these questions. Complete the questions (1–6) with the simple past form.

1   "_____ born?"
    "In 1963."

2   "What subject _____ ?"
    "Science Education."

3   "_____ *National Geographic* TV?"
    "In 1997."

4   "Where _____ ?"
    "In Norway."

5   "When _____ to do a handstand?"
    "When I was five."

6   "_____ performing on your own?"
    "When I was nineteen."

6 **Pronunciation** **simple past irregular verbs**

a Write the simple past form of these irregular verbs. (Check your answers in a dictionary.)

1   bite   _____
2   buy   _____
3   hit   _____
4   do   _____
5   say   _____
6   go   _____
7   fight   _____
8   bring   _____
9   meet   _____

b ▶ **23** Listen and check your answers from Exercise 6a. Write the words you hear in the correct column in the chart below.

/ɛ/	/ɪ/	/ɔ/
said	*bit*	*bought*

4b Survival stories

Vocabulary personal qualities

1 Read the clues below and complete the crossword with words describing personal qualities.

Across

2   happy to wait for other people if necessary

5   An employee who works long hours is very _____ .

6   able to learn and understand things quickly and easily

7   having skill or knowledge from doing something many times

Down

1   behaving in a cheerful and pleasant way toward other people; easy to get along with

3   happy, optimistic, and confident

4   generous, helpful, and thinking about other people's feelings

2 Pronunciation word stress

a ▶ 24 Listen and check your answers from Exercise 1. Underline the syllable that is stressed.

Example:
patient

b ▶ 24 Listen again and repeat.

Reading books and movies of true stories

3 Read the article. Then match the stories (A–E) with the statements (1–7) on page 31. Sometimes more than one story matches a statement.

Survival stories

Some of the best movies and books come from true stories. This is particularly true for stories about mountaineers and explorers. Here are five of the best stories which became books and movies.

A In 1996, Jon Krakauer went to Mount Everest. He wanted to climb the mountain and write about it. However, while he was there, eight people died in terrible weather on the side of the mountain. Krakauer described what happened in his book *Into Thin Air*.

B When a plane was flying over the Andes in 1972, it crashed, but some of the passengers survived. Two Uruguayan men, Nando Parrado and Roberto Canessa, walked for many days across the mountains to get help. Their story became a movie called *Alive*.

C In 1865, while Edward Whymper and his team were climbing the Matterhorn mountain, one of the men fell. As he fell, his rope pulled others down with him. Whymper survived and wrote a book about the events.

D In 1924, the climber George Mallory wanted to be the first person to climb Everest. He never returned, and no one knows if he reached the top. As a result, there are many books about this famous mountaineering mystery.

E While the explorer Ernest Shackleton was sailing around the Antarctic, his ship, *Endurance*, became stuck in the ice. Eventually, Shackleton and his crew left the ship and spent sixteen days crossing 1,300 kilometers (807 miles) of ocean in small boats to the island of South Georgia. Shackleton published his famous story of survival in 1919.

1 This story isn't about any mountains. ____
2 The people in the story were not explorers or mountaineers. ____
3 We don't know if this person achieved his aim. ____
4 Bad weather was the problem in this story. _A_
5 The leader of the team survived in these stories. ____
6 These stories include problems with transportation. ____
7 These stories describe long journeys. ____

Grammar past continuous and simple past

4 Underline any past continuous forms in the article on page 30.

5 Write past continuous sentences using these prompts.

1 The sun / shine / and people / sunbathe / on the beach.
_____
_____

2 We / not / study / when the teacher walked in.
_____
_____

3 We / walk / past the building when the fire started.
_____
_____

4 She / not / think / about her exam results when the envelope arrived.
_____
_____

5 It / not / rain, / so we went for a picnic.
_____
_____

6 Circle the correct options to complete the conversations.

Conversation 1
A: ¹ *Did you see / Were you seeing* all those police cars this morning?
B: No. What happened?
A: They ² *followed / were following* a red sports car, but I don't know if they caught the driver.
B: I ³ *saw / was seeing* on the news that there was a bank robbery, so it was probably something to do with that.
A: I can't believe you ⁴ *didn't hear / weren't hearing* the cars as they went past.
B: I ⁵ *listened / was listening* to music with my headphones, so I couldn't hear anything else.

Conversation 2
A: Sorry I was late this morning. My usual train ⁶ *didn't arrive / wasn't arriving* today, so I had to wait for a later train.
B: So that's why you were fifteen minutes late.
A: Yes. Why? ⁷ *Were you waiting / Did you wait* for me?
B: No, I wasn't. But you were late yesterday. And the day before! It's becoming a problem.

Word focus extra *fall*

7 Look at the forms of the word *fall* in these sentences. Match the sentences (1–4) with the uses and meanings of *fall* (a–d).

1 When did you fall in love with each other? ____
2 I fell off my bicycle and hurt my arm. ____
3 The temperature fell by 5 degrees in an hour. ____
4 The falls are on the other side of this mountain. ____

a to decrease
b to move down to the ground, by accident
c to suddenly have strong feelings for someone
d a place where water moves from a higher to a lower point

8 Complete these sentences with the phrases in the box.

fell asleep	fell by 3%	fell off	fell in love

1 I met my husband in 1998, and we _____ right away.
2 The price of gas _____ this month.
3 My leg hurts! I _____ my skateboard.
4 I find baseball really boring. I _____ while watching the game on TV.

4c Different challenges

1 Vocabulary extra challenges

You are going to listen to an interview with a conservationist. Before you listen, match the words (1–8) with the definitions (a–g). Two words mean the same thing and match one definition.

1 conservationist   5 jungle

_____   _____

2 rain forest   6 meditation

_____   _____

3 expedition   7 determination

_____   _____

4 preparation   8 mental

_____   _____

a   a long journey to find or study something
b   quiet thinking to help you relax
c   an area of land in a tropical region where trees grow very closely together
d   when you don't let anything stop you from achieving your goal
e   a person who works to protect the environment
f   of the mind (i.e., opposite of *physical*)
g   the process of planning and getting ready for something

Listening a walk through the Amazon rain forest

2 ▶ **25** Listen to an interview with Daniel Fanning, the leader of an expedition to the Amazon rain forest. Circle the topics (1–4) he talks about.
1   how to prepare for the rain forest
2   what type of clothing you need
3   dangerous animals in the rain forest
4   the physical and mental sides of walking in the jungle

3 ▶ **25** Listen again. Answer the questions.
1   How long did the expedition last?

    _____

2   Why did Daniel need to test the tents?

    _____

    _____

3   What are the most important things to carry?

    _____

4   How much weight did Daniel lose?

    _____

5   According to Daniel, what personal quality do you need on this kind of expedition?

    _____

Grammar extra *in*, *on*, or *at*

▶ **GRAMMAR *in*, *on*, *at***

- We use *in* with months, years, seasons, and times of the day:
  in February, in 1963, in the spring, in the afternoon
- We use *on* with days and dates:
  on Saturday, on June 29
- We use *at* with times and certain time expressions:
  at 2 p.m., at night

4 Complete the sentences with *in*, *on*, *at*, or – (no preposition).

1   _____ May 1953, Edmund Hillary and Tenzing Norgay became the first men to reach the summit of Mount Everest.
2   _____ the evenings, we cooked dinner over a fire and watched the stars.
3   The two women reached the summit _____ exactly three o'clock that afternoon.
4   The expedition leaves _____ Monday.
5   The rescue team arrived _____ three days later.
6   Roald Amundsen was the first explorer to reach both the North and South Poles. He died in a plane crash _____ June 18, 1928.
7   The two climbers returned safe and well _____ yesterday.
8   The group of explorers arrived home _____ New Year's Eve.

4d True stories

Listening a true story

1 ▶ **26** Listen to a true story about Yossi Ghinsberg's journey through the jungle of Bolivia. Number the events (a–f) in the correct order (1–6).

____ a The four men got lost.
____ b Local people found Yossi.
____ c Yossi and Kevin traveled down the river on a raft.
____ d Yossi fell off the raft.
____ e Four men traveled into the jungle of Bolivia.
____ f Local people found Kevin.

> **raft** (n) /rɑːft/ a simple boat made from pieces of wood tied roughly together

2 Dictation Yossi Ghinsberg

▶ **26** Listen again and complete the story with the words you hear.

[1] _____ , Yossi Ghinsberg started a journey with three other men. They were traveling through the jungle of Bolivia, but [2] _____ , they became lost. [3] _____ , two people in the group—Yossi and Kevin—built a raft so they could travel down the river and find help. [4] _____ they traveled down the river, but [5] _____ they hit a rock. Yossi fell off the raft and swam to shore. [6] _____ Yossi was lost in the jungle, his friend Kevin was luckier. Kevin stayed on the raft, and [7] _____ some local men found him. [8] _____ they searched for Yossi. [9] _____ , [10] _____ , they found him alive. [11] _____ , the other two men never returned.

Real life telling a story

3 Look at the words and phrases you wrote in Exercise 2. Match them with the uses below (a–e).

a refers to days and periods of time:
_____ , _____ ,
_____ , _____ ,

b sequences parts of the story:
_____ , _____ ,
_____

c introduces new and surprising information:
_____ , _____

d introduces good news: _____
e introduces bad news: _____

4 Pronunciation intonation for responding

a ▶ **27** Listen to these sentences. Some speakers sound interested or surprised. Other speakers don't. Circle the phrases with interested or surprised intonation.

1 Why was that?
2 That was a good idea!
3 Oh, no!
4 That was lucky!
5 Wow!

b ▶ **28** Listen to the sentences again. This time the speakers all sound interested or surprised. Repeat the sentences, copying the intonation.

5 Listen and respond responding to good and bad news

▶ **29** Listen to someone telling you a story. Respond to each sentence with an expression from the box. Then compare your response with the model answer that follows.

| Wow! | That was a good idea! | Why? |
| Oh, no! | That was lucky! | |

I had a terrible trip into work this morning.

Why?

4e A story of survival

1 Writing skill structure your writing

a Read the story below. The parts of the story (A–E) are in the wrong order. Number the parts in the correct order (1–5).

> **A** _____
>
> I felt confident when I started walking early on the first day. I had a tent, and enough food and water for three days. Unfortunately, toward the end of Day One, I lost the trail. Also, the battery on my phone ran out, so I couldn't look at the map.

> **B** _____
>
> I slept for another night, and then I got up early on Day Three before the sun became too hot. Around noon I was feeling dehydrated, but just as I was starting to panic, I came to the edge of a cliff, and there at the bottom was the Verde River.

> **C** _____
>
> It was a beautiful day and I was on a trip through the Sycamore Wilderness Canyon in Arizona. It's the second largest canyon in the US. However, it isn't very well known—there are no roads or campsites, and sometimes you don't see another person for days.

> **D** _____
>
> It took two hours to climb down the side of the cliff, but eventually I reached the river and drank the water. Further along the river, I found a trail. A day later, I arrived home. I knew I was very lucky to be alive.

> **E** _____
>
> After one or two hours I was still lost and it was getting dark, so I put up my tent. Luckily, it didn't rain, but I didn't sleep well because I was worried. The next day, I walked for hours again in high temperatures. By the end of the day, I only had a bit of water left.

b Cover the story. Match the time expressions (1–8) with the events (a–h). Then read the story again and check your answers.

1   On the first day, _____
2   Toward the end of Day One, _____
3   After one or two hours, _____
4   The next day, _____
5   On Day Three, _____
6   Around noon, _____
7   It took two hours _____
8   A day later, _____

a   he arrived home.
b   he started walking.
c   he was feeling dehydrated.
d   to climb down the cliff.
e   he lost the trail.
f   he was still lost and it was getting dark.
g   he walked for hours.
h   he got up early.

2 Grammar extra adverbs for structure

a Underline these adverbs in the story and notice their position.

also	only	again	still	just	then

b Write the adverb in parentheses in the correct place in each of these sentences.

1   We walked for three hours, and we sat and enjoyed the view. (then)
2   I arrived home as the sun went down. (just)
3   The explorers tried to leave their camp, but the weather was still too bad. (again)
4   After three hours, we were lost. (still)
5   We were three days from anywhere, and we had food and water for one more day. (only)
6   The jungle is very hot. There are many dangerous animals. (also)

Writing a short story

3 Write a short story (100 words) that begins with the words: "We only had food and water for one more day … ." In your story, use six or more adverbs.

Wordbuilding verbs and nouns

1 Complete the sentences with these nouns.

achievement	answer	memory	player
score	solution	study	test

1 Finishing the project on time was a great
_____ .

2 My father works from home in his
_____ .

3 The _____ with number 10 on his
shirt is amazing. What's his name?

4 We spent hours discussing the problem, but we
never came up with a _____ .

5 What's the _____ to this question?

6 I can't go out tonight. I need to review my
notes for my _____ tomorrow.

7 I have a terrible _____ for people's
names. I never remember them.

8 The _____ is 2-1, and there's only five
minutes left in the match.

2 Complete these sentences with verbs formed from
the nouns in Exercise 1.

1 This quiz will _____ your
understanding of the material.

2 He can _____ a Rubik's cube
in less than 20 seconds.

3 Did you _____ 100% on the test?

4 How did you _____ all the words on
the list? I forgot lots of them.

5 It's easier to learn to _____ a musical
instrument when you are young than when
you are older.

6 A: Samuel won his school's talent competition.
B: How did he _____ that?

Learning skills planning your study time

3 Many people learn English in a class with other
people. Having regular lessons at a certain time
helps you learn, but it's also important to study
outside the classroom. Think about how you
can plan your time for studying on your own.
Circle the correct options to make these statements
true for you.

HOW I STUDY

1 My favorite time of day for studying
is *in the morning / in the afternoon /
in the evening.*

2 I think I can spend *about an hour /
between two and three hours /
more than three hours* a week studying
on my own.

3 The best days in my week for studying
are *Monday / Tuesday / Wednesday /
Thursday / Friday / Saturday / Sunday.*

4 The best place for me to study is
*in a particular place in my house /
in a library / in a coffee shop / other.*

4 Now think about these other suggestions for
studying. Answer the questions.

5 This workbook is an important part of
studying. How much of this workbook
can you complete every week?

6 It is useful to read through the Student
Book and your notes after each class.
When will you be able to do this?

7 Most people agree that it is better
to study every day for ten or fifteen
minutes than once a week for an hour
or two. Is it possible for you to work
this way? When could you spend
a few minutes studying every day
(e.g., on the bus to work or during your
lunch break)?

Check!

5 Can you remember what you read or heard about
these places? Try to answer the questions. You can
find the answers in Unit 4 of the Student Book.

Lukla	Kabul	Tehran	Siula Grande
Atafu			

1 Who was in these places in Unit 4 of the
Student Book?

2 What happened to the person or people in
these places?

Unit 5 The environment

5a Recycling begins at home

Vocabulary recycling

plastic wrap

1 Look at these notes from a student's notebook. Complete the rest of the diagram in the same way.

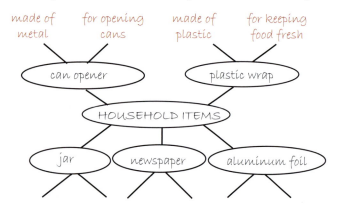

Grammar quantifiers

2 Look at the nouns (1–6). Decide if you can use *a*, *an*, or *some*.

1 _____ banana   4 _____ egg

2 _____ juice   5 _____ milk

3 _____ box   6 _____ carton

▶ **SPELL CHECK plural countable nouns**

- Add *-s* to most countable nouns: *egg* → *eggs*
- Add *-es* to nouns ending in *-ch, -s, -ss, -sh,* and *-x*: *sandwich* → *sandwiches*
- Change nouns ending in *-y* (after a consonant) to *-i* and add *-es*: *city* → *cities*
- Don't change the *-y* to *-i* after a vowel: *key* → *keys*
- Some nouns are irregular: *man* → *men*

---

3 Look at the spell check box. Then write the plural form of these countable nouns. Use a dictionary if necessary.

1 jar   _____

2 bus   _____

3 country   _____

4 holiday   _____

5 woman   _____

6 can   _____

7 box   _____

8 child   _____

9 phone   _____

10 class   _____

11 story   _____

12 cartridge _____

4 Complete the pairs of sentences with the quantifiers.

1 some / any

   a There are _____ cakes on the table.

   b There isn't _____ sugar.

2 any / many

   a I don't have _____ eggs, but I can give you one.

   b I don't have _____ eggs. We'll have to buy some.

3 a lot of / much

   a We have _____ old aluminum foil that we should recycle.

   b We don't use _____ aluminum foil because plastic wrap is better.

4 a few / a little

   a There are _____ ink cartridges in that box.

   b There's only _____ ink in this pen.

5 a few / many

   a I don't get _____ days off for vacation.

   b I have _____ days every year for vacation.

6 a little / much

   a I only get _____ exercise at the gym each week.

   b Do you get _____ exercise?

5 Complete the sentences with these words. Are the sentences true for you?

any	few	lot	many	~~some~~

1 There are ___*some*___ recycling bins in each office.
2 There aren't _____ plastic cups. Everyone has to bring in their own coffee cup.
3 There are a _____ signs in the office to remind people to turn off anything electrical at the end of the day.
4 Some people drive to work, but there aren't _____ places to park. Most people travel by bus or they cycle to work.
5 We use a _____ of paper in the office for printing documents.

Reading reusing household items

6 Read the article about recycling. Match these headings (a–e) with the paragraphs (1–5).

a Items made of paper _____
b Storage items _____
c Plastic bags _____
d House cleaning _____
e Clothing _____

7 Read the article again. Answer these questions.

1 What is better than taking household items to the recycling center?
_____

2 What can you use for cleaning instead of paper towels?
_____

3 What types of storage items are good for reusing?
_____

4 What three uses does the writer suggest for old newspapers?
_____

5 Where can you take old clothes and shoes?
_____

6 What two uses does the writer suggest for old plastic bags?
_____
_____

♻ Recycling

Reusing household items is better for the environment than throwing them away. Reusing requires less energy than collecting household trash or taking it to the recycling center. Here are some ideas for reusing common household items.

1 The next time you don't have any paper towels for cleaning, don't go to the store. Make your own from old cotton shirts, old socks, and old towels. You can clean your car with them, clean the kitchen floor, and dust the furniture. And they're cheap!

2 Wash your glass jars and reuse them to keep small items. In the kitchen, you can store beans, tea, and spices in them. You can also wash yogurt containers as well as other plastic containers and reuse them for food in the fridge.

3 Use your magazines and newspapers for wrapping presents or protecting fragile objects. They can also make good compost. Before you throw away the paper on your desk, ask yourself: *Can I write on the other side first?*

4 Obviously, when your child's old shirts and pants are too small, you can pass them on to smaller kids. Most countries also have second-hand stores, so you can take your shoes and clothes there.

5 We all use too many of these every day and they are hard to recycle, so reuse them for carrying your shopping. When you travel, you can put bottles of liquid in them in case they open.

compost (n) /ˈkɒmpɒst/ a mixture of dead plants and vegetables added to soil to help plants grow

5b What we consume

Vocabulary results and figures

1 Look at the pie and bar charts. Complete the phrases (1–4) with these words.

exactly	just over	nearly	well over

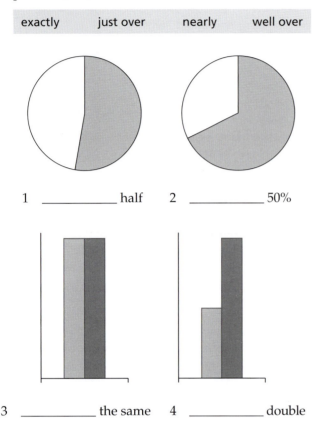

1 _____ half   2 _____ 50%

3 _____ the same   4 _____ double

2 Read the phrases and shade in the pie charts accordingly.

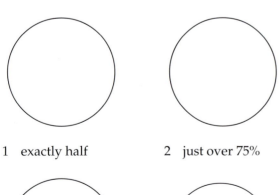

1 exactly half   2 just over 75%

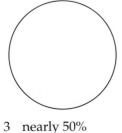
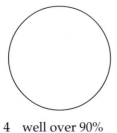

3 nearly 50%   4 well over 90%

Reading understanding a chart

3 This chart compares how often people in different countries recycled their household materials in 2008 and 2009. Complete the statements (1–7) with the correct nationality.

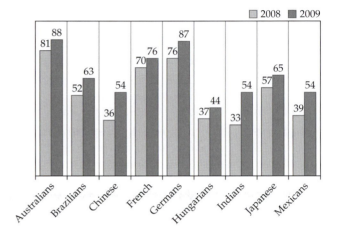

1 In both years, the _Australians_ recycled over eighty percent of the time.

2 The _____ increased their recycling to just over three-quarters of the time in 2009.

3 In 2008, the _____ recycled exactly a third of the time. In 2009, they recycled just over fifty percent of the time.

4 In 2009, the _____ , the _____ , and the _____ all recycled at the same frequency.

5 The _____ increased their rate of recycling by exactly fifty percent.

6 The _____ recycled just over seventy-five percent of the time in 2008 and then well over eighty percent in 2009.

7 The _____ recycled just over a third of the time in 2008 and over forty percent in 2009.

Listening managing the environment

4 ▶ 30 Listen to a news report about environmentally friendly houses. Number the photos (A–C) on page 39 in the order the speaker talks about them (1–3).

carbon emissions (n) /ˈkɑrbən ɪˈmɪʃ(ə)nz/ the amount of carbon dioxide that vehicles or industries put into the air

climate change (n) /ˈklaɪmət tʃeɪndʒ/ a long-term change in the Earth's weather patterns

A _____

B _____

C _____

5 ▶ **30** Listen again and complete these sentences.

1 It's estimated that the construction industry produces around _____ of the world's carbon emissions.

2 The world population is growing, so _____ need houses to live in.

3 The house in Holland is made from _____ . It takes just _____ to build it.

4 Some people are trying to build houses out of _____ , though this isn't a new idea.

5 In about 1905, a man named Tom Kelly built a house made with _____ glass bottles.

6 In London, one _____ has covered a wall with more than _____ plants.

7 Two towers in Milan will have forests on the sides, which will improve Milan's _____ .

8 The forests also protect the people living there from the _____ of the city.

Grammar articles

6 Complete the sentences with *the* or – (no article).

1 Birds eat _____ worms.

2 One day I'd love to visit _____ Amazon rain forest.

3 _____ New Zealand is a country with every type of natural feature.

4 _____ Maldives are a group of islands in the Indian Ocean.

5 My favorite Hollywood actor is staying at _____ Astoria Hotel in London.

6 I don't like driving at _____ night.

7 One of _____ best vacations I had was staying at home for a week!

8 Do you also speak _____ English at home with your family?

9 A: There's a strange car outside our house!
   B: It's _____ same one I told you about earlier.

7 **Pronunciation** /ðə/ **or** /ði:/

▶ **31** Listen to the sentences in Exercise 6 with *the*. Do you hear the pronunciation /ðə/ or /ði:/?

/ðə/ Sentences: _____

/ði:/ Sentences: _____

8 Read this paragraph. An article (*a*, *an*, or *the*) is missing in eight places. Write the missing articles.

Over three hundred million people live in ∧ USA. (*the*)

It is one of world's most multicultural countries.

It used to be part of United Kingdom, but it

became new country in 1776. Washington, D.C.

became capital city, and the president still lives there

in White House today. However, it isn't biggest city.

New York City is bigger, and it's also more popular

with tourists. In particular, they come to see Statue

of Liberty.

5c Trash we produce

Word focus *take*

1 Replace *take* in the sentences (1–6) with these verbs or phrases.

| carry | drink | ~~go by~~ |
| have | last | slow down |

1 Let's **take** a taxi. It's much faster. _____*go by*_____
2 The trip will **take** about three hours. _____
3 **Take your time!** There's no hurry. _____
4 It's time for you to **take** a break. _____
5 You need to **take** 10 ml of this medicine twice a day for two weeks. _____
6 This boat can **take** up to 30 people. _____

2 Complete these sentences in your own words.
1 My commute to work takes _____.
2 I normally take a break _____.
3 It's important to take your time when you _____.
4 It's important to take care when you _____.

Listening one household's trash

3 ▶ **32** Listen to a news report. Answer these questions.

1 What type of news is it about?
_____

2 Which country is it about?
_____

3 What examples of electronic devices does it mention?
_____

4 Does the reporter think recycling electronic devices could have a big effect?
_____

5 What kind of recycling has become successful in this country?
_____

4 ▶ **32** Listen again. Complete this fact sheet with numbers.

American households		
1	Total amount of trash produced = _____ billion kilos	
2	Amount recycled or composted = _____ billion kilos	
Electronic devices		
3	The average American household owns _____ electronic devices.	
4	Households with three or more people own as many as _____ devices.	
5	Recycling one million cell phones could produce _____ kilos of gold.	
Paper recycling		
6	In 2009, the average amount of paper recycled was _____ kilos per person in the US, or about _____ kilos per household.	
7	_____% of American households live near paper recycling projects.	

By Karyn Maier, Demand Media

5d Online shopping

Listening an order by phone

1 ▶ 33 Listen to a customer ordering a garden composter by phone. Complete the order form.

Item number: ¹ _____
Name of item: Garden Composter
Price: ² _____ (including delivery)
Last name of customer: ³ _____
Address: ⁴ _____ Second Avenue, Salem, OR
Type of credit card: ⁵ _____
Card number: ⁶ _____
Email: ⁷ _____

Real life calling about an order

2 ▶ 33 Complete the conversation from Exercise 1 with these questions (a–i). Then listen again and check your answers.

a Can I get your last name?
b Does that include delivery?
c Do you have the item number?
d How can I help you?
e Would you like confirmation by email?
f Is that the garden composter?
g Which credit card would you like to pay with?
h Can I put you on hold for a moment?
i Is there anything else I can help you with today?

S = Sales assistant, C = Customer
S: Good morning. ¹ _____
C: Hi. I'm calling about a product on your website. I'd like to order it, but the website won't let me.
S: One moment … ² _____
C: Yes, it's 7786-P.
S: 7786-P. OK. ³ _____
C: Yes, that's right.
S: Well, I can take your order by phone.
C: OK, but how much does it cost?
S: Hmm. ⁴ _____
C: Sure …

S: Hello?
C: Yes, hello.
S: It's $29.
C: ⁵ _____
S: Yes, it does.
C: OK. I'll order it.
S: Great. I'll need to get some details. ⁶ _____
C: It's Bruce. B-R-U-C-E.
S: And your address?
C: 312 Second Avenue. And that's in Salem, Oregon.
S: ⁷ _____
C: VISA. The number is 4456 8938 9604 9500.
S: Sorry, is that 9500 at the end?
C: Yes, that's right.
S: ⁸ _____
C: Yes, please. My email is bob dot bruce fifty-one at gmail dot com.
S: Let me check: bob dot bruce fifty-one at gmail dot com.
C: That's right.
S: ⁹ _____
C: No, thanks. That's everything.
S: OK. Goodbye.
C: Bye.

3 Listen and respond making an order

▶ 34 You are ordering an item by phone. Listen and respond to the salesperson using this information and your own details. Spell your last name and email address.

Name of item:	Laptop
Item number:	GR897-01
Type of credit card:	Mastercard
Card number:	7558 6799 3647 1023

4 Pronunciation sounding friendly

▶ 35 Listen to the salesperson again. Repeat the expressions with similar intonation so that you sound polite and friendly.

1 How can I help you?
2 Do you have the item number?
3 Can I get your last name?
4 Which credit card would you like to pay with?
5 Can I have the card number?
6 Would you like confirmation by email?
7 Can I have your email address?
8 Is there anything else I can help you with today?

5e Emails about an order

1 Writing skill formal words

These sentences are from two emails. One email is more formal than the other. Write the sentences in the correct order in the two emails below.

a Please email this as soon as possible.
b I'm happy to send you the running shoes.
c But you didn't give me the item no. ☹
d Thanks for placing another order with us!
e We are grateful for your order dated August 30th.
f Please send ASAP.
g We would be delighted to send you the dress immediately.
h However, we require the correct order number.

Hi Hans!

1 *Thanks for placing another order with us!*

2 _____

3 _____

4 _____

All the best,
Malcolm

Dear Ms. Powell,

5 *We are grateful for your order dated August 30th.*

6 _____

7 _____

8 _____

Malcolm Douglas
Customer Care Dept.

---

2 Replace the words in bold in the sentences with these more formal words.

| apologize | 'd be delighted | provide |
| receive | refund | request |

1 I'**m happy** to deliver it today. _____
2 We didn't **get** our order. _____
3 I'm writing to **ask for** a replacement. _____
4 We'**re sorry** for any delay. _____
5 Please **give** your email address. _____
6 When will you **give back** the money? _____

Writing emails

3 Write three different emails between a customer and an online DVD supplier. Use formal language. Follow the instructions in parentheses.

Email 1

(1 Request information about a DVD)
_____
(2 Ask about the price)
_____
(3 Request information ASAP)
_____
_____

Email 2

(4 Thank customer for inquiry)
_____
(5 Say the price is $10)
_____
(6 Add that delivery is included in price)
_____
_____

Email 3

(7 Thank the other person for replying)
_____
(8 Confirm you want to order it)
_____
(9 Ask for information on how to pay)
_____
_____

Wordbuilding hyphenated words

> **WORDBUILDING hyphenated words**
>
> We sometimes use a hyphen to join two or more words. It's always useful to check your dictionary, but here are some examples of when we use a hyphen:
> - two or more words as a noun, e.g., *e-waste, brother-in-law*
> - two or more words as an adjective before a noun, e.g., *out-of-date, second-hand*
> - with a capitalized word, e.g., *anti-English, pro-American*
> - with numbers, fractions, and measurements, e.g., *twenty-one, two-thirds, three-liter plastic bottle*

1 Look at the wordbuilding box. Then write the missing hyphens in these sentences.

1 Please board the plane as we are ready for take off.
2 There's some out of date software here.
3 A lot of people are pro European.
4 Nearly three quarters of the population regularly recycles glass.
5 I only use eco friendly laundry detergent.
6 Do you have an up to date bus schedule?
7 My birthday is on the thirty first of January.
8 My wife's mother is my mother in law.
9 A marathon is a twenty six mile run. That's forty two kilometers.
10 All our products use state of the art technology.

2 Look at an English text (e.g., in a newspaper, on the internet, or in the Student Book) and circle more examples of hyphenated words.

Learning skills using a dictionary (2)

3 Use these exercises to practice your dictionary skills.

1 Look at the noun in this dictionary extract. Is it countable or uncountable? How do you know from the dictionary extract?

> **information** /ˌɪnfərˈmeɪʃən/ noun [U] knowledge or facts about a person or thing

2 Find these five nouns in your dictionary. Are they countable (C), uncountable (U), or both (B)?

> foot _____ information _____ luggage _____
>
> time _____ tooth _____

3 These words all have two or more parts. Find them in your dictionary. Which part of the word or phrase did you look for first?

> out-of-date eco-friendly recycling bin
> can opener user-friendly

4 Find the verb *take* in your dictionary. Answer these questions.
   a How many different meanings does the verb *take* have: fewer than 10? between 10 and 20? more than 20?
   b Find a new collocation or expression with the verb *take*.

5 Look up the verb *reuse* in your dictionary. From the definition, guess the meaning of the prefix *re-*. Then check your answer by looking up the definition of *re-* in your dictionary.

Check!

4 What is the connection between these pairs of words from Unit 5 of the Student Book? Check your ideas by looking back through the unit.

1 Earth ⟷ 30%

_____

2 computers ⟷ e-waste

_____

3 a few ⟷ a little

_____

4 tell ⟷ inform

_____

5 Great Wall ⟷ Green Wall

_____

6 *Plastiki* ⟷ plastic bottles

_____

7 Pacific Ocean ⟷ Garbage Patch

_____

8 Arctic Ocean ⟷ Pacific Ocean

_____

9 Gobi Desert ⟷ Sahara Desert

_____

Unit 6 Stages of life

6a A new life in paradise

1 Vocabulary extra life events

Match the words in box A with the phrases in box B to make collocations. Then complete the sentences (1–4) with the collocations.

A buy	go	start	retire

B a family		their first home
from work		to university

1 I'll _____ when I'm eighteen.
  I want to study physics.
2 It's difficult for young people to _____ now because house prices are so high.
3 Most people _____ in their mid-sixties, but I plan to in my mid-fifties.
4 We decided to _____ once we'd bought a house. Our first child was a girl.

Reading building a dream house

2 Read the article. Match these headings (A–D) with the paragraphs (1–4).

A Preparations before building _____
B The dream _____
C With help from their friends _____
D The obvious choice _____

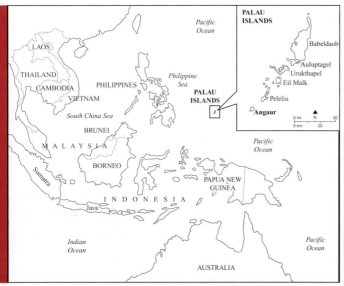

A new **life** in **paradise**

1 Alex Sheshunoff is a writer, and Sarah Kalish was a lawyer. Both had good jobs and an apartment in Iowa City. However, one day they decided to leave it all behind and build a new home for themselves. Most people would be happy to look locally, but Alex and Sarah planned to find a place in paradise to create their new home.

2 For Alex, it was fairly easy to choose an island with everything he wanted. As a scuba diver, Alex first visited the Palau group of islands years ago. He continued to go back from time to time, so this seemed like a good choice. The islands are about 7,500 kilometers (4,660 miles) west of Hawaii and are difficult to reach. They have green forests with interesting wildlife and are surrounded by a blue ocean full of colorful fish. In the end, Alex and Sarah chose one island in particular—Angaur.

3 Angaur is thirteen kilometers (8 miles) around, with a population of about 150 people. Before Alex and Sarah could start building a house, they had to get permission from the head of the island—an 83-year-old woman. She was worried they intended to develop the area for other tourists, but Alex explained that they just wanted to build a simple house. They agreed on the rent of $100 a month for twenty years. The head of the island was happy. She said, "Angaur welcomes you."

4 Then the real work began. Alex and Sarah didn't want to pay for a construction company, so they taught themselves about building. Some friends from Iowa went out to help. In return, they got a free vacation by the beach. The local people of Angaur also worked for the couple, and after many months of hard work and a final visit from the head of the island, their dream house was ready.

3 Read the article again. Answer these questions.

1 Where does the writer think most people would plan to build a new house?
_____

2 Why was it easy for Alex to choose the location?
_____

3 How far are the islands from Hawaii?
_____

4 What are the good things about the islands?
_____
_____

5 How many people live on Angaur?
_____

6 Who gave Alex and Sarah permission to build the house?
_____

7 How much was their rent per month?
_____

8 What did their friends get in return for helping to build the house?
_____

Grammar infinitive forms

4 Underline 12 examples of *to* + base verb in the article on page 44.

5 Match the beginnings of the sentences (1–6) with the endings (a–f).

1 Turn the key _____
2 For dinner, they plan _____
3 Use a dictionary _____
4 Go to Egypt _____
5 Go to university _____
6 I need to go to the bank _____

a to find the translation.
b to take us to a restaurant.
c to unlock the door.
d to see the Pyramids.
e to take out some money.
f to get a degree.

6 Complete the conversation with the infinitive form of these pairs of words.

afraid / move	difficult / keep	easy / make
great / live	nice / see	sad / see

A: Hi. It's ¹ _____*nice to see*_____ you again after all these years. It's been such a long time.
B: Yes, it has. But it's really ² _____ in contact with everyone.
A: Yes, it is. And we were so ³ _____ you leave. Remind me—where did you move to?
B: Australia. We moved there five years ago.
A: Really? Five years ago! I'd be
⁴ _____ such a long way from my friends and family.
B: Actually, it was ⁵ _____ new friends. We're very happy there. And it's
⁶ _____ in a hot country with beaches and a beautiful coast.

7 Circle the correct verb form to complete the sentences.

1 I'm happy *help / to help / helping* you with your homework.
2 You can't *throw / to throw / throwing* the ball forward in rugby.
3 We want *meet / to meet / meeting* at six o'clock.
4 Are you good at *play / to play / playing* tennis?
5 Do you feel like *go / to go / going* out later?
6 I'm studying Chinese *get / to get / getting* a job in Beijing.

8 Pronunciation sentence stress

▶ 36 Listen to these sentences. Then practice saying them. Stress the underlined words.

1 <u>Pleased</u> to <u>meet</u> you.
2 <u>Nice</u> to <u>see</u> you.
3 It's <u>great</u> to <u>be</u> here.

9 Complete these sentences in your own words.

1 I'm always happy to _____
_____ .

2 It's hard to _____
_____ .

3 I think people are crazy to _____
_____ .

6b Special occasions

Vocabulary celebrations

1 Complete the text about festivals around the world with these words.

bands	candles	costumes	fireworks
floats	masks	parades	

Festivals around the world

St. Patrick's Day

On March 17ᵗʰ, Ireland celebrates Saint Patrick's Day. There are ¹ _____ down the streets and people ride on ² _____ .

MassKara Festival

Every October in Bacolod City in the Philippines, thousands of people go to the MassKara Festival wearing ³ _____ and ⁴ _____ .

Bonfire Night

On November 5ᵗʰ in the UK, people light fires and set off ⁵ _____ into the night sky.

Santa Lucia Day

On December 13ᵗʰ, Swedish people celebrate the festival of Santa Lucia. Traditionally, girls wear white dresses and a crown with ⁶ _____ on top.

Teuila Festival

This festival in Samoa lasts two weeks. There are colorful decorations hanging in the streets and ⁷ _____ playing music.

Listening planning a celebration

2 ▶ **37** Listen to a group of people planning a party. Circle the correct option (a–c) to answer each question.

1 What is the reason for the party?
   a a birthday
   b an anniversary
   c a retirement

2 Where do they decide to hold the party?
   a in the office
   b at a restaurant
   c at Rosemary's home

3 Who do they plan to invite?
   a only work colleagues
   b family and friends
   c they can't decide

4 What present are they going to buy her?
   a a book   b a cake   c a plant

3 ▶ **37** Listen again. Answer the questions.

1 Why does one person not want to have the party in the office?

_____

2 Is Zeno's located near the office?

_____

3 What is on the menu there?

_____

4 How many people do they need to book the restaurant for?

_____

5 What time is the party?

_____

6 Why can't one person be there at five o'clock?

_____

7 Why do they decide to give Rosemary a plant as a present?

_____

8 Why do they stop the meeting?

_____

Grammar future forms: *going to*, *will*, and present continuous

4 Circle the correct options to complete part of the conversation from Exercise 2.

C: What time [1] *is everyone going to meet /*
will everyone meet there?
A: Right after work. At five o'clock.
B: But [2] *I'll work / I'm working* late on Friday.
A: Well, between five and six then. We also need to get her a present.
C: What [3] *are we going to give / are we giving* her? Oh, I know! She loves plants, and I think [4] *she's going to spend / she's spending* a lot of time gardening when she retires.
A: Good idea. A plant, then.
C: And I think we should have a special cake as well.
A: [5] *Is the restaurant going to make /*
Will the restaurant make us one?
C: Um, I'm not sure. [6] *I'm going to ask / I'll ask* them.

5 Circle the correct response (a or b) for each sentence.

1   Oh, no! I've forgotten my wallet!
a   Don't worry. I'll pay.
b   Don't worry. I'm going to pay.

2   Can you help me later?
a   Sorry, I'll help Max later.
b   Sorry, I'm going to help Max later.

3   Are you in the parade this afternoon?
a   No, but I'll watch it at three o'clock.
b   No, but I'm going to watch it at three o'clock.

4   Do you want to come to the nightclub with me this evening?
a   Sorry, but I'll see a movie.
b   Sorry, but I'm going to see a movie.

5   Let's go to the movies tonight.
a   Good idea. I'll see what's playing.
b   Good idea. I'm going to see what's playing.

6 Pronunciation contracted forms

▶ **38** Listen to four sentences. Circle the sentence you hear (a or b).

1   a   Don't worry. I'll pay.
b   Don't worry. I will pay.

2   a   I'm going to help Max later.
b   I am going to help Max later.

3   a   Shelley's coming too.
b   Shelley is coming too.

4   a   He'll be eighteen years old tomorrow.
b   He will be eighteen years old tomorrow.

▶ **GOING TO or PRESENT CONTINUOUS**

You can often use either form to talk about plans and arrangements in the future, e.g., *We're meeting in the café at five. = We're going to meet in the café at five.*

When you use the present continuous to talk about the future, you normally need a future time reference, e.g., *We're meeting in the café **at five**.*

When you don't use a future time expression, the present continuous often refers to the present time, e.g., *We're meeting in the café (now).*

---

7 Look at the grammar box above. Rewrite the sentences below using the present continuous. Does it change the future meaning?

1   We're going to meet my friends later today.
We're meeting my friends later today.   ✓

2   We're going to call you back.
We're calling you back.   ✗

3   Is the teacher going to tell us the answer?
_____

4   Are you going to go to the festival tomorrow?
_____

5   They're going to decorate the float.
_____

6   The parade is going to pass by my house this afternoon.
_____
_____

7   Why is everyone going to wear a mask?
_____

8 Dictation plans for a celebration

▶ **39** Listen to someone describing their plans for a celebration. Write the words you hear.

_____
_____
_____
_____
_____
_____
_____
_____

6c Coming of age

Listening an ancient ceremony

1 ▶ **40** Listen to a documentary about an Apache ceremony. Number the pictures (A–E) in the order the speaker describes them (1–5).

___ A

___ B

___ C

___ D

___ E

2 ▶ **40** Listen again. Complete the summary of the ancient ceremony.

An ancient ceremony

An Indian tribe called the Mescalero Apaches have a special ceremony every year that starts on
¹ _____ . It is a ceremony for young Apache ² _____ .

At the beginning, each family makes food for many guests, and the men build a special tepee. The girls will live in this for ³ _____ days. On the first day, the girls run toward the ⁴ _____ and around a basket of food four times. Each time represents the four stages of their life: infant, ⁵ _____ , teenager, and adult woman. Then they live in the tepee.

On the last night, the girls have to dance for over ⁶ _____ hours. In the morning, the girls come out of the tepee with white clay on their ⁷ _____ . They remove the clay, and the tepee falls to the ground. The girls receive a new name and celebrate their new position—as ⁸ _____ .

clay (n) /kleɪ/ wet material from the ground which you can use to make bowls, cups, and plates

Word focus *get*

3 Complete the phrases with *get* in the sentences with these words.

back	married	presents	ready	together	~~up~~

1 What time do you get *up* in the morning?
2 What time do you get _____ from work?
3 Hurry and get _____ . It's time to leave.
4 I try and get _____ with my family at least once a year.
5 What _____ did you get from everyone for your birthday?
6 We plan to get _____ after we both finish university, but it won't be a big wedding.

6d An invitation

Real life inviting, accepting, and declining

1 ▶ **41** Listen to two telephone conversations. Answer these questions.

Conversation 1

1   When does Sonia want to meet Mihaela?

　　_____

2   Which restaurant are they going to meet at?

　　_____

3   Who does Mihaela want to bring?

　　_____

Conversation 2

4   Why does Philippe decline Mihaela's invitation?

　　_____

5   What does Mihaela suggest?

　　_____
　　_____

6   Does Philippe accept the invitation in the end?

　　_____

2 ▶ **41** Complete the excerpts from the conversations in Exercise 1 with these expressions. Then listen again and check your answers.

Do you want	How about	I'd like
I'd love to	That sounds	That would
It's very nice	Why don't you	Yes, OK

Conversation 1

Sonia:　　I'm at work so I can't talk long.
　　　　　¹ _____ to meet after work?
Mihaela:　² _____ .
Sonia:　　³ _____ meeting outside my
　　　　　office? We could go to that new Lebanese
　　　　　restaurant on Main Street.
Mihaela:　⁴ _____ great. Oh, I've just
　　　　　remembered. I have a friend from France
　　　　　staying. He's doing a language course at
　　　　　the college near me.
Sonia:　　That's OK. ⁵ _____ invite
　　　　　him as well?
Mihaela:　⁶ _____ be great. I'll do that.

Conversation 2

Mihaela:　I'm meeting a close friend of mine
　　　　　tonight, and ⁷ _____ you to
　　　　　meet her.
Philippe:　⁸ _____ of you to ask,
　　　　　but I'm busy tonight. I have an exam
　　　　　tomorrow, so I need to study at home.
Mihaela:　Are you sure? We're going to eat at a
　　　　　new restaurant. We could get home
　　　　　early, or you could study first and come
　　　　　out later.
Philippe:　Honestly, ⁹ _____ , but I'm
　　　　　afraid this exam is really important.

3 Listen and respond responding to an invitation

▶ **42** Listen and respond to two different invitations. For each one, first decline the invitation and give a reason. Then accept it. Compare your responses with the model answers that follow.

> Do you want to see a movie tonight?

> Sorry, I can't because I'm going to a soccer match tonight.

4 Pronunciation emphasizing words

a ▶ **43** Listen to these sentences. You will hear a speaker saying each sentence in two ways. Which has the most natural sentence stress? Write *1* or *2*.

1   I'm really sorry, but I can't.　*1*
2   That'd be great. _____
3   It's so nice of you to ask. _____
4   I'd love to. _____

b Practice saying the sentences.

6e An annual festival

1 Writing skill descriptive adjectives

a Replace the words in **bold** in the sentences with these more descriptive adjectives.

colorful	dull	exciting
massive	miserable	tasty

1   I sat down with the fishermen to eat a **nice** meal of fresh fish from the sea. _____

2   The women were wearing **red, yellow, and blue** dresses for the party. _____

3   The parade through the streets was long and a little **boring** after a while. _____

4   The mountains outside our hotel were **big** and had snow on the top. _____

5   The children didn't seem **unhappy** even though they had very little food. _____

6   The bus trip from my hotel to the airport wasn't very **interesting**. _____

b Match the sentences (1–6) from Exercise 1a with topics (a–f) in the chart below.

a clothes _____	b food ___1___
c people _____	d transportation and towns _____

e festivals _____	f nature and
	      geographic features
	      _____

c Imagine you are writing a description which includes the six topics (a–f) in Exercise 1b. Which of these adjectives would be useful for each topic? Write them in the chart. You can use some adjectives for more than one topic. Use a dictionary to help you.

amazing	attractive	beautiful	delicious
enormous	friendly	fun	polluted
pretty	speedy	uncomfortable	unhealthy

Writing a description

2 A student has prepared this plan for a description of an annual festival in her town. Use the notes and write a short description (one paragraph).

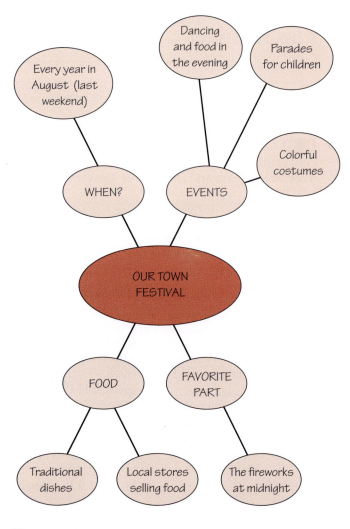

3 Now plan and write a similar short description of an event that happens in your town or city once a year.

Wordbuilding synonyms

1 Cross out the word in each group that isn't a synonym. Use a dictionary to help you.

1 sorry   apologetic   ~~worried~~
2 fast   warm   speedy
3 scary   awful   frightening
4 good-looking   strong   handsome
5 tall   thin   skinny
6 hide   find   discover
7 see   notice   touch
8 relaxed   happy   cheerful

Learning skills assessing your own progress

2 You are halfway through this course. Think about your progress so far. Answer the questions in the self-assessment questionnaire on the right. Write a comment to explain each answer.

Check!

3 Look at these words from Unit 6 of the Student Book. Write the words in the correct category in the chart below.

candle	feijoada	fireworks
toddler	Hamar	middle-aged
Port-of-Spain	colleagues	Venice

A place	
A type of dish or something you can eat	
Something that gives light	
A stage of life	
A group of people	

Assess your progress

1 How would you describe your progress in English in the course so far?

Excellent ☐   Good ☐
Satisfactory ☐   Not very good ☐

Comment on your answer:

_____
_____
_____

2 Which areas would you like to work on most for the rest of the course?

Speaking ☐   Grammar ☐
Listening ☐   Writing ☐
Pronunciation ☐   Vocabulary ☐
Reading ☐

Comment on your answer:

_____
_____
_____

3 Which types of activities in class do you think are most useful for you?

_____
_____
_____

4 What's one thing you would like more of in this course?

_____
_____

5 What's one thing you would like less of in this course?

_____
_____

6 What question do you have for your teacher about the rest of the course? Write it here and ask your teacher to reply.

_____
_____

Audioscripts

Unit 1

▶ 02

A: Hey, here's a quiz to test your stress levels. You said that you're stressed all the time, so let's find out.

B: I don't really have time for this. I have to finish this report.

A: That's just my point. You need to take a break at lunchtime.

B: OK, then. Ask me.

A: Do you often worry about money?

B: Um, no, not really. I don't have time!

A: OK. So we'll say once a month. Two. Do you have problems sleeping? Never, sometimes, or always?

B: Well, it depends. Lately, no, but sometimes I stay awake thinking about work and other things.

A: OK, so that's … sometimes. Three. Do you find it difficult to concentrate?

B: Well, at work I do because people interrupt me all the time with things like quizzes!

A: I think you're fine, so I'll answer "rarely." And the last one. Describe your lunchtimes. Do you do work while you're eating your lunch?

B: Always. I do things like reply to my emails.

A: OK, I'll circle "a." But you know, you should leave the office and go for a walk instead.

B: Well, that's great in theory, but I have so much work to do!

▶ 03

a   I'm driving to the city.
b   What are you doing?
c   She's leaving now.
d   It isn't raining.
e   Why are they running?
f   We aren't stopping anywhere.

▶ 04

I usually get up at about seven o'clock and go running for half an hour. Then I feel ready for the day. I leave the house at about eight thirty and arrive at the hospital by nine. Currently, I'm seeing lots of children with the flu. After work, I often walk home. Sometimes friends come over for dinner, but I need eight hours of sleep a night, so I'm always in bed by eleven o'clock.

▶ 05

I = Interviewer, D = Dunn

I: What makes you feel happy? Is it food that tastes delicious? A painting that looks beautiful? Or maybe just going to a café and having coffee with friends? To tell us what makes us happy, I'm talking to psychologist Elizabeth Dunn. So, Ms. Dunn, I know that you do a lot of research into happiness, and in particular into money and happiness. So tell us, how much money does someone need to be happy?

D: It's a complicated question. Some people think money is the most important thing in the world for happiness. That's definitely not true. Some people think that money doesn't make you feel happier. That's also not true.

I: So maybe the question isn't about money, but how people spend it.

D: Yes. To find out, we did an experiment with some students. We gave them twenty dollars in the morning, and one group spent it on themselves and the other group spent it on someone else. By the end of the day, the people who spent it on others were happier.

I: So, we need to think about the way we use money.

D: Yes, this is something a lot of people find. Spending money on experiences that you enjoy—like visiting a new country or going to a concert to listen to your favorite musician—can make you happier than spending money on things.

▶ 07

D = Doctor, P = Patient

D: How do you feel today?

P: Not very well. I have a terrible sore throat.

D: I see. Let me have a look. Open wide. Yes, it's very red in there.

P: I also have a bad cough.

D: Do you have a stomachache?

P: No, not really.

D: Do you have a temperature?

P: I don't think so. I don't feel hot.

D: Let me check it … Yes, it's a little high. Do you have anything for it?

P: I bought some pills at the pharmacy, but they didn't do any good.

D: Well, take this prescription to the pharmacy. You need to take some different pills. They are good for your throat. Take one every four hours. You need to rest for a couple of days, and try drinking lots of water.

P: OK. Thank you.

D: If you still feel sick after a few days, come back and see me, but I think it's the flu.

▶ 08

F = Friend, MA = Model answer

F: I have a headache.

MA: You need to take some pills.

F: I have a sore throat.

MA: Try drinking some hot water with lemon and honey.

F: I have a bad back.

MA: Stay in bed for a couple of days.

F: I feel sick.

MA: You need to see a doctor.

F: I have a runny nose.

MA: Take this medicine. It's good for the flu.

▶ 09

P = Patient, R = Receptionist

P: Hello, I'm George Braun. I have an appointment with Doctor Swan.

R: Good morning. As it's your first time visiting Doctor Swan, we'll need some personal information. Can I ask you a few questions?

P: Sure. Go ahead.

R: So it's Mr. G. Brown. Do you have a middle initial?

P: Yes, it's P for Paul. But my last name is Braun, not Brown. That's B-R-A-U-N.

R: Oh, OK. Sorry about that. And what's your date of birth?

P: June 7th, 1967.

R: June 7th, 1967. Got it. And I need your address.
P: Um, I'm staying with a friend at the moment, so I don't have a permanent address.
R: Well, can I get your friend's address? We can update it later when you move.
P: OK. It's 21 Carter Street. That's C-A-R-T-E-R street. The zip code is 50530.
R: Great. Do you have a daytime contact number?
P: Yes, the best number is my cell phone number. That's 915-555-7618.
R: And now I have a few questions about your health. If you don't want to answer them, that's OK. Overall, how would you describe your general health? Good? Just OK? Not good?
P: Overall, it's good I think. I exercise a lot and I eat well.
R: How much exercise do you do each week?
P: I go running three times a week. So that's about three hours of exercise per week.
R: Good. Anything else in addition to running?
P: Well, I go swimming sometimes. And I like hiking on the weekends with my friends.
R: So running, swimming, and hiking. OK. I'll give you this form and you can give it to the doctor when you see him.

Unit 2

▶ 10

1   They don't have to win.
2   He can win the game.
3   Do you have to wear a helmet?
4   A player can't hit the ball twice.

▶ 12

Kristi Leskinen is a famous skier. She loves skiing all over the world, but her favorite place is Mammoth Mountain in the USA. She's good at other sports such as kayaking, but she doesn't like running or going to the gym. Recently, she was in a TV show called *The Superstars*. In the show, famous athletes compete in different sports that they don't normally do. Kristi won the competition. But now it's winter again, so she needs to go back to the mountains and start training. This year, she'd like to win a lot more medals.

▶ 13

Free diving is the general word for any type of underwater sport without breathing equipment, so you have to take a deep breath before you go underwater. One of the most competitive types of free diving is when a diver goes deep under the water. A Swedish woman named Annelie Pompe holds the world record in free diving. She went down 126 meters into the Red Sea with no air.

Annelie loves being in the sea and she likes swimming without a lot of equipment. She spends every weekend training in the sea, and before a competition, she trains for about twenty hours a week. She also has time for other sports, and these help her prepare for free diving. For example, she does yoga in the morning because it helps her relax. She also goes running, does some weightlifting, and goes cycling.

Annelie also enjoys mountain climbing. In 2011 she became the first Swedish woman to climb Mount Everest from the north side. For Annelie, adventure is about going to the deepest and to the highest parts of the world.

▶ 14

A: Hey, this looks interesting.
B: What?
A: This leaflet for fitness classes at the gym. Are you interested in doing something like that?
B: Maybe. But I'm not very good at sports.
A: But this isn't competitive. It's for getting fit. This one sounds good: Boot Camp. What about joining that?
B: What is Boot Camp?
A: It's like the army. You have someone who tells you what to do. I think we should do it. It starts at six o'clock.
B: Great. So we can go after work.
A: No, it's six in the morning.
B: What?! I hate getting up early. What about doing something that starts later?
A: Well, there's one at lunchtime. It's called Zumba. It's a kind of dance class, I think.
B: I don't like dancing.
A: Really? It looks pretty fun.
B: What about something after work?
A: There's a Pilates class. It doesn't give an exact time, but it says it's after work.
B: Well, I'd prefer that to Boot Camp or dancing.
A: Yes, it looks good.

▶ 15

F = Friend, MA = Model answer
F: Are you interested in Boot Camp?
MA: No, I wouldn't like to do it.
F: Really? You'd enjoy it. It's before work at six in the morning.
MA: I hate getting up early.
F: What about joining the Zumba class? It's kind of like dancing.
MA: I'm not very good at dancing.
F: Hmm... Pilates sounds good. You should do it with me.
MA: Yes, I'd prefer that to Boot Camp or Zumba.

Unit 3

▶ 18

Last year in India, people bought around 1.5 million new cars. This number will probably go up to three million a year in the next few years. That's how quickly the Indian economy is changing. Many people in the big cities are richer than ever, and they want to spend their money on new products. Most of the money is still in the big cities. There is still a lot of poverty in the villages and countryside.

Now the government hopes a new road in India can help improve India's economy. The Golden Quadrilateral road, or GQ, connects the country's four biggest cities: Delhi, Mumbai, Chennai, and Kolkata. The goal is for the road to carry business from the giant cities to the smaller and poorer villages and the other half of India's population.

The GQ is nearly 6,000 kilometers long and is the most high-tech highway in the world. At the administration headquarters in Delhi, you can watch thousands of vehicles moving around the country on a computer screen. If there is a problem anywhere on the highway, electronic sensors tell the headquarters, and engineers instantly drive there.

When you drive on the GQ, there is every kind of vehicle. There are animals pulling carts, motorcycles, lines of old trucks, and fast-moving modern cars. Sometimes the road goes right through the middle of a city, so there are often traffic jams and pedestrians trying to cross the six lanes. Industry is also growing along the new highway. When a large company opens a factory, lots of other smaller factories and offices also open. Trucks then drive and make deliveries all over India along the new highway. The Golden Quadrilateral is a symbol of India's future.

▶ 20

Conversation 1
A: Hi. Do you go downtown?
B: Which part?
A: Near the movie theater.
B: Yes, we stop in front of it.
A: Great. Can I have a round-trip ticket, please?

Conversation 2
A: I'd like a first-class ticket to the city, please.
B: That's forty-two dollars.
A: Here you are. Which platform is it?
B: Platform 12.

Conversation 3
A: How many bags are you checking in?
B: Two.
A: I'm afraid your ticket only includes one bag. You'll have to pay an extra twenty dollars for that one.
B: Oh, OK. Can I pay by credit card?
A: Sure.

Conversation 4
A: It's just up here on the right. You can drop me off over there.
B: I can't stop there. It's a bus stop. But here is fine.
A: OK. How much is that?
B: That's thirteen dollars and thirty cents.
A: Here you go.

▶ 21

MA = Model answer
Person 1: What kind of train ticket would you like?
MA: Round-trip, please.
Person 2: Are you checking in any bags today?
MA: Yes, this one.
Person 3: Are you paying by credit card?
MA: No, with cash.
Person 4: It's three dollars and twenty cents. Do you have the exact change?
MA: Yes, I do. Here you are.
Person 5: Where does your train leave from?
MA: Platform 9.

▶ 22

Message 1
Get on the Number 68 bus from the bus stop outside your house. Take it to the train station. Catch the first train and get off at Union Square Station. Then call me.

Message 2
My flight is late and I'm still in Chicago. Don't wait for me at the airport. I'll catch the bus downtown and walk to your apartment. See you later.

Message 3
Chris wants to meet us tonight, so please call him and tell him where. And send me the address of the restaurant as well. What time do you want to meet?

Unit 4

▶ 24

Across: 2 patient, 5 hardworking, 6 intelligent, 7 experienced
Down: 1 friendly, 3 positive, 4 kind

▶ 25

I = Interviewer, D = Daniel
I: Could you walk through the jungle and survive? One man who knows all about this is rain forest conservationist Doctor Daniel Fanning. Daniel led a team through the Amazon rain forest. Together, they walked for six months. Daniel is here today to explain how he prepares for this kind of expedition.
D: Well, I think preparation is probably the most important part of any expedition. I spent about three months getting ready for this trip. I tested equipment for the walk. For example, I needed to know if the tents could survive the difficult conditions in the rain forest.
I: So, how much did you have to carry in the end? For example, how much clothing did you take?
D: Humans don't need a lot of clothes in the rain forest. It's hot, so I recommend shorts and a good raincoat.
I: But don't you need good walking boots?
D: The problem is that you get lots of sand, mud, and water inside the boots—especially when it rains, which is nearly all the time. So a pair of sandals is fine. Food and water are the most important things to carry.
I: I was wondering about that. What did you eat?
D: Food like rice is good, but you lose a lot of weight when you walk. I lost about twenty kilos.
I: And one final question. We've talked about the physical side of walking in the jungle, but what about the mental side?
D: Well, you're with other people, but you're also on your own for long periods of time. But that's good for you, I think. It's like a kind of meditation. I also think a journey like this is about determination. I knew that nothing would stop me from reaching the end. So the mind is as important as the body on an expedition.

▶ 26

One day, Yossi Ghinsberg started a journey with three other men. They were traveling through the jungle of Bolivia, but after a few days, they became lost. In the end, two people in the group—Yossi and Kevin—built a raft so they could travel down the river and find help.

For some time they traveled down the river, but suddenly they hit a rock. Yossi fell off the raft and swam to shore.

While Yossi was lost in the jungle, his friend Kevin was luckier. Kevin stayed on the raft, and luckily some local men found him. Then they searched for Yossi. Amazingly, after three weeks, they found him alive. Sadly, the other two men never returned.

F = Friend, MA = Model answer
F: I had a terrible trip into work this morning.
MA: Why?
F: My car broke down on the highway.
MA: Oh, no!
F: I called the police immediately.
MA: That was a good idea!
F: Luckily, while I was calling, a police car drove past and stopped to help me.
MA: That was lucky!
F: Anyway, they called the garage to get my car and then they brought me to work!
MA: Wow!

Unit 5

▶ 30

It's estimated that the construction industry produces around 40% of the world's carbon emissions, which cause climate change. At the same time, the world population is growing, so more people need houses to live in and buildings to work in. So how can we balance the need for houses and the need to reduce carbon emissions?

One way is to design new types of houses that aren't bad for the environment. Take the cardboard house from Holland. That's right. I said cardboard. The house is made from thick, strong cardboard, with wood on the inside. It comes in pieces 1.2 meters wide, or almost four feet, so it's easy to transport and it takes just one day to build it. The cardboard is covered in plastic, so the house stays up in the rain. It can last for decades, and at the end of its life, you can recycle most of the components.

Another recyclable material is glass, and some people are trying to build houses out of glass bottles, though this isn't a new idea. In about 1905, a man named Tom Kelly built a house made with 51,000 glass bottles. The air inside the bottles is an excellent way to keep the temperature comfortable.

And if you don't like the idea of living under cardboard or glass, then you could choose a more traditional building, but have "living walls" on the outside. In London, one hotel has covered a wall with more than 10,000 plants; and in Milan in Italy, they are growing forests on the sides of two towers. The tall buildings will have 900 plants and trees on the sides, which will improve Milan's air quality. The forests also protect the people living there from the noise and heat of the city.

▶ 32

Now, on to environmental news. A new report contains some interesting facts and figures on how much garbage a house in the United States produces. Together, American households produce 243 billion kilos of trash. About 82 billion kilos of this—that's about a third—was made into compost or recycled. For individual households, that means about 0.7 kilograms was recycled out of nearly two kilos.

As for electronics, the average American household owns 24 electronic devices. These mostly include cell phones, music players, laptops and computers, and digital cameras. Households with three or more people often own as many as 32 devices, while smaller households own around 17 devices. Recycling more of these items could have a big effect. For example, recycling one million cell phones can produce 3,500 kilos of gold. Recycling one million computers helps reduce greenhouse gas emissions. It's about the same as taking 16,000 cars off the road.

In 2009, the amount of paper recovered from recycling averaged 150 kilos per person in the United States, or about 380 kilos for each household. Paper recycling has become successful in the US because about 268 million people, or about 87 percent of American households, now have paper recycling projects nearby.

▶ 33

S = Sales assistant, C = Customer
S: Good morning. How can I help you?
C: Hi. I'm calling about a product on your website. I'd like to order it, but the website won't let me.
S: One moment ... Do you have the item number?
C: Yes, it's 7786–P.
S: 7786–P. OK. Is that the garden composter?
C: Yes, that's right.
S: Well, I can take your order by phone.
C: OK, but how much does it cost?
S: Hmm. Can I put you on hold for a moment?
C: Sure. …
S: Hello?
C: Yes, hello.
S: It's twenty-nine dollars.
C: Does that include delivery?
S: Yes, it does.
C: OK. I'll order it.
S: Great. I'll need to get some details. Can I get your last name?
C: It's Bruce. B–R–U–C–E.
S: And your address?
C: 312 Second Avenue. And that's in Salem, Oregon.
S: Which credit card would you like to pay with?
C: VISA. The number is 4456 8938 9604 9500.
S: Sorry, is that 9500 at the end?
C: Yes, that's right.
S: Would you like confirmation by email?
C: Yes, please. My email is bob dot bruce fifty-one at gmail dot com.
S: Let me check: bob dot bruce fifty-one at gmail dot com.
C: That's right.
S: Is there anything else I can help you with today?
C: No, thanks. That's everything.
S: OK. Goodbye.
C: Bye.

▶ 34

How can I help you?
Do you have the item number?
Can I get your last name?
Which credit card would you like to pay with?
Can I have the card number?
Would you like confirmation by email?
Can I have your email address?
Is there anything else I can help you with today?
Goodbye.

Unit 6

▶ 37

A = Boss, B = Colleague 1, C = Colleague 2
A: OK, everyone. Thanks for coming. The reason I wanted to keep the meeting secret was because, as you know, Rosemary is retiring from the company on Friday, so we're going to have a small party for her.
B: Sorry, but where are we going to have a party? The office is big, but it isn't a very good place to … well, you know, to have fun.

C: That new restaurant next door is good. It's called Zeno's. They serve pizzas and Italian food.
B: It is good. I went there last week.
A: Sounds good. There are going to be about twenty of us. Can someone call the restaurant and make a reservation?
C: I'll do it! I'll call them this afternoon and see what they say.
A: Great.
B: So, who are we going to invite? Just staff? What about wives, husbands, boyfriends, girlfriends?
A: I think only the people she works with.
C: What time is everyone going to meet there?
A: Right after work. At five o'clock.
B: But I'm working late on Friday.
A: Well, between five and six then. We also need to get her a present.
C: What are we going to give her? Oh, I know! She loves plants, and I think she's going to spend a lot of time gardening when she retires.
A: Good idea. A plant, then.
C: And I think we should have a special cake as well.
A: Will the restaurant make us one?
C: Um, I'm not sure. I'll ask them.
A: Great. Anything else?
B: Look out! Rosemary's coming back from her lunch.

▶ 38
1 Don't worry. I'll pay.
2 I am going to help Max later.
3 Shelley is coming too.
4 He'll be eighteen years old tomorrow.

▶ 39
Tomorrow our town will be two hundred years old. We are going to have a huge celebration. We plan to have a street parade with costumes and masks. Local musicians are going to play traditional music, and at midnight there are going to be fireworks!

▶ 40
In the US state of New Mexico, the Mescalero Apache Indian tribe prepares for a special ceremony every year. Beginning on July 4th, a group of young Apache girls will spend four days taking part in an ancient ritual that tests their strength and character. By the end of the ritual, they will be women. Preparations begin with each girl's family making food for many guests and members of the local tribe.

Nearby the men start to build a special tepee. The girls will live in this for the four days.

The ritual begins on the first day at sunrise. The girls run toward the morning sun, and then they run around a basket of food four times. Each time represents the four stages of their life: infant, child, teenager, and adult woman.

Then they live in the tepee, where they don't have much food. This is part of their test of strength. They must not show any emotions during this period. On the last night, they start to dance. This dance lasts over ten hours through the night and they cannot stop.

On the final morning, the girls come out of the tepee for the last time. They have white clay on their faces, which they slowly wipe off. The tepee falls to the ground, and they are now women. The girls receive a new name, and their family and friends come to the girls to celebrate their new status—as women.

▶ 41
Conversation 1
S = Sonia, M = Mihaela
S: Hi, Mihaela. It's me, Sonia.
M: Hi, Sonia. How are you? How was your vacation?
S: Great, thanks. But I'm at work so I can't talk long. Do you want to meet after work?
M: Yes, OK.
S: How about meeting outside my office? We could go to that new Lebanese restaurant on Main Street.
M: That sounds great. Oh, I've just remembered. I have a friend from France staying. He's doing a language course at the college near me.
S: That's OK. Why don't you invite him as well?
M: That would be great. I'll do that.

Conversation 2
P = Philippe, M = Mihaela
P: Hello?
M: Philippe. It's Mihaela.
P: Oh, hi, Mihaela.
M: Where are you?
P: I'm about to go to class.
M: Oh, OK. I'll be quick. I'm meeting a close friend of mine tonight, and I'd like you to meet her.
P: It's very nice of you to ask, but I'm busy tonight. I have an exam tomorrow, so I need to study at home.
M: Are you sure? We're going to eat at a new restaurant. We could get home early, or you could study first and come out later.
P: Honestly, I'd love to, but I'm afraid this exam is really important.

▶ 42
F = Friend, MA = Model answer
Invitation 1
F: Do you want to see a movie tonight?
MA: Sorry, I can't because I'm going to a soccer match tonight.
F: How about going to the movies tomorrow night instead?
MA: OK. That'd be great.

Invitation 2
F: Would you like to come to a friend's wedding party?
MA: It's very nice of you to ask, but isn't it only for your friend's family and close friends?
F: But I'd like to take you. You'd enjoy it.
MA: OK. I'd like that very much. Thank you.

Life Combo Split 3A, 2nd Edition
John Hughes, Helen Stephenson,
Paul Dummett, David Bohlke

Vice President, Editorial Director:
  John McHugh

Publisher: Andrew Robinson

Senior Development Editor: Derek Mackrell

Associate Development Editor: Yvonne Tan

Director of Global Marketing: Ian Martin

Senior Product Marketing Manager:
  Caitlin Thomas

Media Researcher: Rebecca Ray,
  Leila Hishmeh

Senior IP Analyst: Alexandra Ricciardi

IP Project Manager: Carissa Poweleit

Senior Director, Production:
  Michael Burggren

Production Manager: Daisy Sosa

Content Project Manager: Beth McNally,
  Tan Jin Hock

Manufacturing Planner:
  Mary Beth Hennebury

Art Director: Brenda Carmichael

Cover Design: Lisa Trager

Text Design: emc design ltd.

Compositor: DoubleInk Publishing Services

American Adaptation: Kasia McNabb

For product information and technology assistance, contact us at
Cengage Learning Customer & Sales Support, cengage.com/contact

For permission to use material from this text or product,
submit all requests online at **cengage.com/permissions**
Further permissions questions can be emailed to
permissionrequest@cengage.com

Combo Split 3A + App: 978-1-337-90814-6
Combo Split 3A + App + My Life Online: 978-0-357-04794-1

National Geographic Learning
20 Channel Center Street
Boston, MA 02210
USA

National Geographic Learning, a Cengage Learning Company, has a mission to bring the world to the classroom and the classroom to life. With our English language programs, students learn about their world by experiencing it. Through our partnerships with National Geographic and TED Talks, they develop the language and skills they need to be successful global citizens and leaders.

Locate your local office at **international.cengage.com/region**

Visit National Geographic Learning online at **NGL.Cengage.com/ELT**
Visit our corporate website at **www.cengage.com**

STUDENT BOOK CREDITS
Although every effort has been made to contact copyright holders before publication, this has not always been possible. If notified, the publisher will undertake to rectify any errors or omissions at the earliest opportunity.
Text: p10 Adapted from: (from question 2 onwards) http://ngm.nationalgeographic.com/2010/05/sleep/quiz/sleep#/sleep; p11 Adapted from: http://ngm.nationalgeographic.com/2010/05/sleep/max-text; p12 Adapted from: http://ngm.nationalgeographic.com/ngm/0511/feature1/index.html; p13/181 Adapted from: http://ngm.nationalgeographic.com/ngm/0511/sights_n_sounds/index.html; p15 Adapted from: http://www.natgeotraveller.in/web-exclusive/web-exclusive-month/this-is-your-brain-on-nature/; p22 Adapted from: http://americanfestivalsproject.net; p23 Adapted from: http://americanfestivalsproject.net; p24 Quotations, www.brainyquote.com; p27 Adapted from: http://ngm.nationalgeographic.com/2008/09/wrestlers/guillermoprieto-text called "Bolivian Wrestlers"; p34 Adapted from: http://news.nationalgeographic.com/news/energy/2011/11/pictures/111123-amazing-transportation-ideas/; p37 Adapted from: http://news.nationalgeographic.com/news/special-features/2014/08/140808-london-cabbies-knowledge-cabs-hansom-uber-hippocampus-livery/; p39 Adapted from: http://ngm.nationalgeographic.com/2008/04/kolkata-rickshaws/calvin-trillin-text; p44 Adapted from: https://www.itdp.org/2017-sustainable-transport-award-winner/; p46 Adapted from: http://adventure.nationalgeographic.com/adventure/adventurers-of-the-year/2016/vote/pasang-lhamu/; p47 Adapted from: http://www.nationalgeographic.com/field/explorers/reza/; p48/183 Source: Daily Telegraph 22.10.07. http://www.telegraph.co.uk/news/features/3634463/Joe-Simpson-My-journey-back-into-the-void.html; p51 Adapted from: http://solution-dailybrainteaser.blogspot.co.uk/2015/09/classic-matchstick-puzzle.html; p56 Adapted from: http://www.nationalgeographic.com/adventure/adventurers-of-the-year/2015/aleksander-doba/; p58 Adapted from: http://ngm.nationalgeographic.com/2008/01/high-tech-trash/carroll-text/1; p60 Adapted from: http://www.theguardian.com/environment/2016/may/18/portugal-runs-for-four-days-straight-on-renewable-energy-alone; p60/184 Adapted from: http://www.economist.com/news/international/21613334-vast-tree-planting-arid-regions-failing-halt-deserts-march-great-green-wall; p61 Source: BBC Focus, April 2016, page 64; p63 Source: http://ngadventure.typepad.com/blog/plastiki/; p64 Source: http://www.tecoart.com/; p71 Adapted from: http://www.nationalgeographic.com/adventure/photography/adventure-dreams/road-trip/lessons-learned.html; p72 Adapted from:

Printed in China by CTPS
Print Number: 02   Print Year: 2019

Charles W. Berry/National Geographic Creative; 24 (b) © Ed Kashi/National Geographic Creative; 28 © Brady Barr/National Geographic Creative; 29 © Sindre Lundvold/Barcroft Media/Getty Images; 30 Royal Geographical Society/Alamy Stock Photo; 32 © Elena Kalistratova/iStockphoto; 33 © Tal Karaso; 36 Lee Foster/Alamy Stock Photo; 37 © Mincemeat/Shutterstock.com; 39 (t) © Yvonne Witte/Wikkelhouse; 39 (m) © Sharad Raval/Shutterstock.com; 39 (b) © Eugenio Marongiu/Shutterstock.com; 40 © Joseph Sohm/Shutterstock.com; 41 © Jerome Whittingham/Shutterstock.com; 46 Thomas Cockrem/Alamy Stock Photo; 49 Art Directors & TRIP/Alamy Stock Photo.

Illustrations: 22, 48 Kevin Hopgood/Kevin Hopgood Illustration; 23 Lumina Datamatics; 31 Matthew Hams; 44 David Russell.

ACKNOWLEDGEMENTS

The *Life* publishing team would like to thank the following teachers and students who provided invaluable and detailed feedback on the first edition:

Armik Adamians, Colombo Americano, Cali; Carlos Alberto Aguirre, Universidad Madero, Puebla; Anabel Aikin, La Escuela Oficial de Idiomas de Coslada, Madrid, Spain; Pamela Alvarez, Colegio Eccleston, Lanús; Manuel Antonio, CEL – Unicamp, São Paolo; Bob Ashcroft, Shonan Koka University; Linda Azzopardi, Clubclass; Éricka Bauchwitz, Universidad Madero, Puebla, Mexico; Paola Biancolini, Università Cattolica del Sacro Cuore, Milan; Lisa Blazevic, Moraine Valley Community College; Laura Bottiglieri, Universidad Nacional de Salta; Richard Brookes, Brookes Talen, Aalsmeer; Alan Broomhead, Approach International Student Center; Maria Cante, Universidad Madero, Puebla; Carmín Castillo, Universidad Madero, Puebla; Ana Laura Chacón, Universidad Madero, Puebla; Somchao Chatnaridom, Suratthani Rajabhat University, Surat Thani; Adrian Cini, British Study Centres, London; Andrew Clarke, Centre of English Studies, Dublin; Mariano Cordoni, Centro Universitario de Idiomas, Buenos Aires; Kevin Coughlan, Westgate Corporation; Monica Cuellar, Universidad La Gran Colombia, Colombia; Jacqui Davis-Bowen, St Giles International; Maria del Vecchio, Nihon University; Nuria Mendoza Dominguez, Universidad Nebrija, Madrid; Robin Duncan, ITC London; Christine Eade, Libera Università Internazionale degli Studi Sociali Guido Carli, Rome; Colegios de Alto Rendimiento, Ministry of Education of Peru; Leopoldo Pinzon Escobar, Universidad Catolica; Joanne Evans, Linguarama, Berlin; Scott Ferry, UC San Diego ELI; Juan David Figueroa, Colombo Americano, Cali; Emmanuel Flores, Universidad del Valle de Puebla; Bridget Flynn, Centro Colombo Americano Medellin; Sally Fryer, University of Sheffield, Sheffield; Antonio David Berbel García, Escuela Oficial de Idiomas de Almería, Spain; Lia Gargioni, Feltrinelli Secondary School, Milan; Roberta Giugni, Galileo Galilei Secondary School, Legnano; Monica Gomez, Universidad Pontificia Bolivariana; Doctor Erwin Gonzales, Centro de Idiomas Universidad Nacional San Agustin, Peru; Ivonne Gonzalez, Universidad de La Sabana; J Gouman, Pieter Zandt Scholengemeenschap, Kampen; Cherryll Harrison, UNINT, Rome; Lottie Harrison, International House Recoleta; Marjo Heij, CSG Prins Maurits, Middelharnis; María del Pilar Hernández, Universidad Madero, Puebla; Luz Stella Hernandez, Universidad de La Sabana, Colombia; Rogelio Herrera, Colombo Americano, Cali; Amy Huang, Language Canada, Taipei; Huang Huei-Jiun, Pu Tai Senior High School; Carol Humme, Moraine Valley Community College; Nelson Jaramillo, Colombo Americano, Cali; Jacek Kaczmarek, Xiehe YouDe High School, Taipei; Thurgadevi Kalay, Kaplan, Singapore; Noreen Kane, Centre of English Studies, Dublin; Billy Kao, Jinwen University of Science and Technology; Shih-Fan Kao, Jinwen University of Science and Technology, Taipei; Youmay Kao, Mackay Junior College of Medicine, Nursing, and Management, Taipei; Fleur Kelder, Vechtstede College, Weesp; Waseem Khan, YBM; Dr Sarinya Khattiya, Chiang Mai University; Lucy Khoo, Kaplan; Karen Koh, Kaplan, Singapore; Susan Langerfeld, Liceo Scientifico Statale Augusto Righi, Rome; Hilary Lawler, Centre of English Studies, Dublin; Jon Leachtenauer, Ritsumeikan University; Eva Lendi, Kantonsschule Zürich Nord, Zürich; Michael Ryan Lesser, Busan University of Foreign Studies; Evon Lo, Jinwen University of Science and Technology; Peter Loftus, Centre of English Studies, Dublin; José Luiz, Inglês com Tecnologia, Cruzeiro; Christopher MacGuire, UC Language Center, Chile; Eric Maher, Centre of English Studies, Dublin; Nick Malewski, ITC London; Claudia Maribell Loo, Universidad Madero, Puebla; Malcolm Marr, ITC London; Graciela Martin, ICANA (Belgrano); Michael McCollister, Feng Chia University; Erik Meek, CS Vincent van Gogh, Assen; Marlene Merkt, Kantonsschule Zürich Nord, Zürich; Jason Montgomery, YBM; David Moran, Qatar University, Doha; Rosella Morini, Feltrinelli Secondary School, Milan; Christopher Mulligan, Ritsumeikan University; Judith Mundell, Quarenghi Adult Learning Centre, Milan; Cinthya Nestor, Universidad Madero, Puebla; Nguyen Dang Lang, Duong Minh Language School; Peter O'Connor, Musashino University, Tokyo; Cliona O'Neill, Trinity School, Rome; María José Colón Orellana, Escola Oficial d'Idiomes de Terrassa, Barcelona; Viviana Ortega, Universidad Mayor, Santiago; Luc Peeters, Kyoto Sangyo University, Kyoto; Sanja Brekalo Pelin, La Escuela Oficial de Idiomas de Coslada, Madrid; Itzel Carolina Pérez, Universidad Madero, Puebla, Mexico; Sutthima Peung, Rajamangala University of Technology Rattanakosin; Marina Pezzuoli, Liceo Scientifico Amedeo Avogadro, Rome; Andrew Pharis, Aichi Gakuin University, Nagoya; Hugh Podmore, St Giles International, UK; Carolina Porras, Universidad de La Sabana; Brigit Portilla, Colombo Americano, Cali; Soudaben Pradeep, Kaplan; Judith Puertas, Colombo Americano, Cali; Takako Ramsden, Kyoto Sangyo University, Kyoto; Sophie Rebel-Dijkstra, Aeres Hogeschool; Zita Reszler, Nottingham Language Academy, Nottingham; Sophia Rizzo, St Giles International; Gloria Stella Quintero Riveros, Universidad Catolica; Cecilia Rosas, Euroidiomas; Eleonora Salas, IICANA Centro, Córdoba; Victoria Samaniego, La Escuela Oficial de Idiomas de Pozuelo de Alarcón, Madrid; Jeanette Sandre, Universidad Madero, Puebla; Bruno Scafati, ARICANA; Anya Shaw, International House Belgrano, Argentina; Anne Smith, UNINT, Rome & University of Rome Tor Vergata, Italy; Courtney Smith, US Ling Institute; Suzannah Spencer-George, British Study Centres, Bournemouth; Students of Cultura Inglesa, São Paulo; Makiko Takeda, Aichi Gakuin University, Nagoya; Jilly Taylor, British Study Centres, London; Caroline S. Tornatore, Austin Community College; Juliana Trisno, Kaplan, Singapore; Ruey Miin Tsao, National Cheng Kung University, Tainan City; Michelle Uitterhoeve, Vechtstede College, Weesp; Anna Maria Usai, Liceo Spallanzani, Rome; Carolina Valdiri, Colombo Americano, Cali, Colombia; Keith Vargo, Westgate Corporation; Gina Vasquez, Colombo Americano, Cali; Andreas Vikran, NET School of English, Milan; Helen Ward, Oxford, UK; Mimi Watts, Università Cattolica del Sacro Cuore, Milan; Yvonne Wee, Kaplan Higher Education Academy; Christopher Wood, Meijo University; Kevin Wu, Hangzhou No.14 High School; Yanina Zagarrio, ARICANA.